Surviving the Game of Life

9 8 7 6 5 4

ISBN: 978-1-933630-94-6

Author: Damon Dorsey Rozier
with Virginia Chatterton

Library of Congress Cataloging-in-Publication Data

Rozier, Damon Dorsey.
Surviving the game of life / Damon Dorsey Rozier with Virginia Chatterton.
  p. cm.
ISBN 978-1-933630-94-6
1. Rozier, Damon Dorsey—Health. 2. Quadriplegics—Rehabilitation—
United States—Biography. I. Chatterton, Virginia. II. Title.
RC406.Q33R694 2010
362.4'3092—dc22
[B]

                    2009044571

Produced by Vestal Creative Services
Cover and interior design: MK Bassett-Harvey

Printed in the United States of America

VESTAL
CREATIVE
SERVICES

an imprint of
Harding House Publishing Service, Inc.

Surviving the Game of Life

Damon Dorsey Rozier
With
Virginia Chatterton

VESTAL
CREATIVE
SERVICES

We have all become familiar with inspirational stories of people who overcome incredible adversity to regain success and happiness, and discover inner strength. The easy access to many forms of media can make such stories seem almost routine. They are not. Spinal cord injury is one of the most traumatizing conditions that can affect a person because of the resulting paralysis, loss of feeling, incontinence, sexual dysfunction, pain and psychological damage that it imposes. In a twenty year career as a physician specializing in the treatment of people with spinal cord injuries, I have seen many people regain a good quality of life and many others who have been defeated by such injuries. It is exceptionally rare to see someone who achieves a higher level of function and quality of life than they had before such an overwhelming tragedy. *Surviving the Game of Life* is the first hand account of Damon Rozier, a truly remarkable man who has reached a better place by overcoming physical, psychological and social challenges that are nearly insurmountable. Further, he regularly uses his experiences to bring laughter, courage and strength to others who are facing such challenges. From my vantage point as Damon's physician of eleven years, I am amazed by his journey and am proud to have been a small part of it.

—*Adam B. Stein, MD*
Chairman, Department of Physical Medicine and Rehabilitation
The North Shore–Long Island Jewish Health System

FOREWORD

This book has been written about the life of Damon Dorsey Rozier. The first few chapters were spoken into a recording device while he was recovering from an accident prior to 1999. From that time on, Virginia Chatterton has written the remainder of the book. There have been readings, re-readings, and much editing throughout the book. Phone interviews and emails with family members, friends, and a therapist have contributed to the content. Many names have been omitted, as it isn't names that are important but rather the survival of one who has surmounted major obstacles to succeed. This is a testimonial to the idea that when the odds seem against you, perseverance, determination, support from those who believe in you, and most of all, faith in God, will bring you to more than Survival in this Game of Life.

CONTENTS

CHAPTER 1

Early Years

Swirling through life, we all go through many journeys. Some of the paths we choose are exciting and adventuresome, but some of the paths lead to destruction of the self. This life about which you will learn has crisscrossed many avenues of pain, of trials and tribulations, of ecstatic moments, and of exhilaration. This life goes from one of self-destruction to a life rebuilt on a firm foundation with a future that holds so much promise.

When we are young, we take many chances and life can become just a matter of surviving. I have been a survivor of many journeys in life. Even when times seemed to threaten my survival, I have picked myself up and trudged forward to the next segment of my life.

Right now, I am at an incredible peak in my life's journey. When the call came to get a flight to Hollywood, and be ready to tape a segment for a nationally televised comedy show, this mind of mine was in disbelief! Me! Is this real? How did this happen? I have had a dream, just as many others in history have had dreams, to succeed, to change the world, to change lives, and to change how people believe. My dream has been to make this journey of life the best I can make it. It must be more than survival. This dream is big, but I know that I can do it for myself, for my children, for all those I hold dear. Nothing is going to stop me. Nothing will stand in my way which I cannot surmount. Everything takes time, effort, patience, and determination.

Now, let me take you back to where the journey of my life began, Brooklyn, New York. This borough is one of dirt, real filth, many gun-wielding inhabitants and abundant crime. My birth occurred on a sunny afternoon in August, the tenth day, and the year was 1967. Brookdale Hospital was along a major street with cars whizzing by any hour of the day or night. At six and three quarter pounds, twenty-one inches long, I came into the family as the third and youngest child of Hugh Dorsey and Elicia Thompson Rozier. When I was born, my mother was pleased to have another son. She had prayed that this baby would look like his father and have his personality. Her prayers were answered, but little did she know how often this might haunt her later. The resemblance to my father was definitely there. My dad was a man of the streets and spent many hours with his friends in the park near the apartment complex.

According to my mother, I was the most active of her children, with a pleasant and happy countenance. She recalls that I smiled all the time and was such a good child. I walked at eleven months, exploring everything in sight, climbing this, climbing that, examining how toys were put together, banging pots and pans and generally trying to see of what my world was made. Talking came quite early too and progressed along normal patterns of speech. At age one and a half, my legs and body moved with the rhythm of any style of music, I am told. People loved to see me rotate around and around, wiggling this way and that in time to the music. The more I danced, the better I became, dancing with my siblings, my mom or just alone, wherever and whenever the rhythm caught my mood.

It seems that I had no fear of anything as a child or as a young adult. Mom recalls quite vividly that one week she had me to the hospital three times because of incidents in which I had fallen and had what appeared to my mom as serious injuries. She has always said that I was into everything and had a daredevil attitude.

People described all of us children as being very mannerly, "even the youngest one." Please and thank you were easily remembered, holding doors for family or when out shopping was never a problem. Even at the age of two and a half or three, I really did not like sharing my toys. Mother noticed that my older brother would give up his toys to a kid who might want to play with them, but with me, I would hold on to whatever it was and shout, "That's mine. You can't have it!" There was no willingness to give up any toy without a tug, a pull and perhaps a punch or two to hang on to what was mine. Seems like I had a short fuse way back then or maybe I just believed that what was mine was mine to keep and nobody else should or could have it.

My brother, Andre is the oldest of my siblings and looks the most like our father. He has always been a bit taller. His personality has been more introverted, but always the nice guy who has chosen his friends very carefully. Cross Andre and you lose his friendship and kind heartedness forever. He never drank and never smoked. He appeared to always do everything right but he could find trouble. He tells of times he did mischievous acts about which mom never knew. One time he and his friends took the subway to the Bronx and did not go to school. It was annoying and induced jealousy within my soul for all the positive attention Andre received. He has utilized many talents and has been a DJ, sews well and makes good money as a tailor. He was always so perfect in everyone's eyes, the golden boy who continues to have a halo, perhaps because he is a smooth guy, very motivated for success. He started his own company, Havoc Enterprises, which is the name of the clothing line he has been developing and the boxing business he promotes.

Tanya is the middle child of the family, the loud and boisterous sister. Tanya was quite intelligent but never obtained the education which she could have had. Her energy level was never the same as her brothers. She seemed to need much more rest than we did. Her love for a good time and to party was of uppermost importance to her life. She and I were the ones who often got into some kind of trouble. Tanya has grown, now, a mother of a son and daughter. She has grown and changed and is much more goal-oriented in life.

Looking back on my life, there was constantly the need to exert myself, to be noticed when my brother or sister was around. This is not all that unusual in any family. My personality was more of an extroverted guy, charismatic, a party animal, but leaned toward making many negative choices. Many words have been used to describe me as a child and as an adult. Inquisitive, perceptive, charming, handsome, likable, moving, giving and loved by the family. Andre and I both enjoyed participating in sports and also watching and cheering for the teams or individuals we supported. Smooth and motivated for success describe me now. I always have wanted to learn but in school, dyslexia caused some of my learning problems. Simply stated, dyslexia is an impairment or condition which interferes with learning to read. My method of recall was mostly as an auditory learner. Those things which were spoken, I could learn and remember easily. When phonics was being taught as the method of learning to read, that was great. However, trying to match the printed symbols of the vowels, blends, digraphs, and all other combinations of letters which were to be visually recognized was most difficult for me. There were times that my motivation to learn was low, especially as a teen. I was much more interested in girls, how they looked, and applied my energy and personality to attract them to me. Today psychologists would say that my social intelligence quotient was high. I could speak well to people and they were charmed by my smile. The family has had a warm spot for me most of my life for much the same reason as my peers. People who meet me for the first time find it easy to have conversation.

Another side of me developed during the early years. I could be described as rebellious, violent, argumentative, adventuresome, a "devil may care" attitude. "It is my way or no way" if someone crossed me. This part of me was not, and is not, what most people saw or would want to see! Over the years, I have learned to control much of this attitude. Generally, the rebelliousness now seems to surface if I feel that I am being personally violated.

My father died when I was a very little boy. I have sketchy details on what really happened when he was murdered in Brooklyn. It has been said that he was stabbed in the leg during a bar fight and that he bled to death. Apparently he did not get to the hospital in time to save his life. From what I have been told, he always tried to protect his family and made sure that nobody disrespected his family. He was known to be a good provider in those years when he was married to my mother. Mom has always said that we had all that we needed.

Later, my mother remarried and this man was a police officer who had three children from a previous marriage, two boys and a girl. We were pretty cool, but they had some funny ways and so did we. Adjusting to one another was not all that easy. I felt that my mother's husband picked on me as a child. He was a very strict man and our house had rules that this new man enforced to the extreme. Being in on time was one rule and cleaning the house was another. What was so upsetting was that my mother allowed this man to beat me while the other siblings did not get a beating when they disobeyed.

One of my uncles was the same age as me. We did lots of things together, some of which were considered stupid by our parents. Once we were trying to climb up the side of a building and I fell down, cutting my nose. Yes, my uncle was like a best friend. We could have been compared to the Little Rascals as we pretty much did everything together. We would go out on the porch at night and talk about the girls. It was cool! Once I recall talking with him about some girls as we walked across the street, when he called, "Look out! Look out!" I looked up and I got hit with a bat right between my eyes at the bridge of my nose. It took eight stitches to sew it up. My uncle dragged me back across the street and all I can remember is my grandfather getting in a cab with me, pressing a cloth down hard on the area to try and stop the bleeding. When I came back from the hospital I went to the kid's house and I didn't feel as upset when I left, seeing that he got the beating he deserved.

There were about five of us in the neighborhood who were friends, almost like family. We all could eat or sleep at one another's house. Our activities together involved some very mischievous behavior. Once I recall crawling around in the nearby poster factory just to see what we could get away with. We did it for a kind of entertainment since we didn't have the kind of video games and individual hand held games which kids have today. Another time, we broke into the bus depot just for the kicks and to say that we managed to do it and not get caught. We were kids with little motivation to do anything positive at this age. Nobody was encouraging us to be involved in any worthwhile activities. There were no jobs to earn money either.

My grandfather was a strict Panamanian man. He did not let us get away with much of anything. I remember once when my uncle and I had a fight, my grandfather came out and beat us so badly that we never fought again. My grandmother was always protecting the children from my grandfather. She thought he was much too strict and should not use such brutal physical force. She was a wonderful cook and she used her passion for cooking to smooth over whatever harsh words my grandfather had spoken, often having us come to eat lunch or dinner with her. My grandmother never raised a hand to us. Memories of my grandmother are just beautiful pictures. She always had a plate of food for any of our friends when they came into her home. If ever I had a problem and wanted someone to listen to me, I just had to go to my grandmother. She would lend an ear and make me feel like everything would be OK.

During my early school years, I did not do as well as was expected because it was thought that I had this eye problem, and I definitely did not want to wear glasses. I really do not think that I had an eye problem. The doctor said I did have an eye problem when I was tested and my mom agreed but I made up a lot of the answers because I was that rebellious kid. There wasn't much I really liked or wanted to do. It didn't make much sense either as I was only making my own life worse than it ever needed to be. I didn't want to do the work and had trouble learning for reasons which were not defined at that time. Perhaps the schools were so over crowded and I was a student who fell through the cracks. I truly had an attitude about going to school. Everyone loved me among teachers and other staff members, but I just hated being at school. There was nothing enjoyable about learning. NOTHING! In spite of this bad attitude, I managed to pass and see it now as having been pushed through each grade with no mastery of the material to be learned. It reminds me of the present initiative of No Child Left Behind. The difference today is that there are many programs to help a child succeed. Actually, the best part of elementary school was recreation time or recess as it was sometimes called. That was fun. The game we all loved was Cocolevio. We played in teams or groups and each group protected an area. When guys came into the area, you grabbed them and had to say, "Cocolevio, Cocolevio, 1, 2, 3, 1, 2, 3." They had to go stand on your side and somebody had to get in to free your men. If you caught all of their men, then you were on the opposite side coming in.

My memory of Junior High School was that it was very rough. The first school I went to was a bad school. When I first got there, a guy had snatched my cap. I chased him through the hallway and was clothes lined by a kid who seemed to be waiting for me. He told me to give him all my money and when I said I had no money, he grabbed my pocket and ripped it. There was a thin little dime there and he took it. That was kind of scary for a guy who had been protected previous to that experience. By this time in my life I was rather chunky, not a small guy. I actually think I was quite fat. That did not help my situation. However, I did adapt well and quickly to my surroundings. Going to the lunchroom was a job in itself. Kids would take your lunch, your lunch money, or just try to get you involved in a fight. Where was the supervision? Why was this sort of thing allowed to take place? I do not have the answers to those questions which still plague my mind. Next, I was transferred out to another intermediate school. My mother hoped that it would be a better placement for me. It too was a rough place. They assigned me to a special education class because they thought I had a difficult time learning when really I had a lot of social and emotional problems at school. I got along well with adults but those rough kids made me very angry. Now I not only had a problem at home but school was horrible. It was a stigma for me being in a special class. I was very stressed about my life at home. Therefore, I was not applying myself to the academic tasks. For some kids maybe there is a major dysfunction of some sort, but I do not recall ever being evaluated nor do I remember receiving any help from guidance counselors. In spite of those unfair circumstances, I made the honor roll, was in the school orchestra (I played the flute) and participated in several Junior High School shows. In addition, I could sing well and was in a choral group. I actually sang a duet at a spring performance. Music was a way I could escape the tragedy of my circumstances.

The prankster in me surfaced during the early teen years. My mother's husband had the car parked near the apartment building and I wanted to go see this girl. So, getting the keys was easy but my knowledge of the girl's exact residence was sketchy. My dog, Tiffany, was traveling with me. Suddenly, the gas needle registered empty and with no money in my pocket, the next best thing would be to snatch a purse and run. A cop saw what happened and caught me as my legs had traveled fast but not fast enough up to the train station. A visit to the police station was in order and my parents were called. This was BIG trouble. Being a minor, this was now a record. My parents were not pleased and were going to leave me there and take the dog! They changed their mind but there was quite a beating in store for me. Probably my mother's husband's cop badge was helpful at the station.

High school was definitely a new experience. By this time in a teen's life, peer approval and attitudes are well established. You tend to think that you know it all and that parents are the last to have any sense of your maturity. How could they possibly know what you are thinking? Most teens have a tendency to share with their friends rather than discuss any problems with their parents. In spite of my attitude, I did quite well my first year in high school. I really became very popular with the girls during my sophomore year. Going into school, girls would be huddled, whispering, and looking at me. It was quite apparent that they were discussing me. Frequently, a girl would come over and ask for my phone number or send someone else of the group to ask for the number. It was quite important to me to be popular. There was a field in back of the school where people hung out whenever possible. Some of the students found it a great place to smoke while others mainly were there to talk or to "make out." The school was close to Coney Island, so there was a group of us who would cut class and ride on over to the Amusement Park, hang out on the boardwalk and have one big party while we should have been in class. Even though there was the rebellious side to me, I truly did not get into fights in high school. I had a crew who ran with me and if I had any problems, the "crew" would handle everything. Since I had people who were selling weed at the school, there was this one guy who just never paid attention to the where, when and who of any sales. This one time in particular, I had told him not to sell any that day and he did not listen. Therefore, the crew was summoned and pushed him into the bathroom where they beat on him to make him remember who was the boss of these deals. I truly cut class on a regular basis and it was amazing that I managed to pass that sophomore year. The teachers were somewhat afraid of me as they knew I had weapons on me. I would stash the weed, knives, and guns in various lockers of my friends. Security guards were cool with me as they bought weed from me also. There were no metal detectors in those days. Nobody searched you. I carried the drugs in a pouch fastened around my waist.

When classes were dismissed for the day, classrooms were not locked. It was easy to go to the math class or the home economics classroom and have sex with my girlfriend. I had a blast in school, like one great party time. The lunch room was a popular place to have a hilariously fun time. There were lots of little groups and each one loved to have me join them as they knew what I was doing. Bonding with lots of people was my aim and this was something done very well. In spite of all my lack of interest in the academics, there was a part of me that decided to begin locking down to pass the grades as there was no way that I would tolerate being held back from my group and crew of friends. No way! I would sooner drop out than have that happen. Then where would I really be?

The teachers during my Senior year really helped a lot to keep me in school. I was still dealing with drugs but partying less. That year there was a ski trip which was incredible. I had never gone skiing before but everyone thought I had. Some of my white brothers took me to the top of the mountain and we all were sniffing cocaine. They were wearing the waterproof ski outfits and I was in a sheep skin coat which was popular then. Halfway down the slope, I fell and my jacket was soaked. It quickly froze and made me realize it was not so cool to be out there and not prepared for the consequences of falling and rolling down the slope. Back at the hotel, my supply of weed was gone as the maid service must have desired to get high that day too.

Dewey Day was quite special as this was when the school shut down all classes for a day of games and contests similar to a field day. Other schools came and seemed to have lots of beautiful girls. There always was a dance contest and of course that is where I could shine and indeed put on quite a show. "Set If Off" was one of the break dance songs to which I could dance like you never saw anyone gyrate. The girls would scream and yell for more. They were crazy for the way I could dance.

I wrote earlier about the strict rules of my stepfather. My mother seemed to back him up with these rules of living in their house. Once, the guys and I were hanging out and I had an eight o'clock curfew. Because I got in at five after eight, I was put on punishment for two weeks. This seemed unfair to me. I also thought that I was being treated differently than my brother and sister. My sister had few problems in this man's eyes and my brother was always treated better than I was treated. Once we were in the room and my mother's husband came in. Andre had been caught stealing from Toys R' Us and I recall that my mother's husband hit Andre one time. Andre turned around and said, "You are not my father. You are not going to be hitting on me." It was a great scene because he turned around, sat down, and they had a chat. Later, when I had a similar incident, I tried the same tactic as Andre had used but it didn't work for me. There was no chat, and my reference to his not being my father seemed to trigger such anger in him that he was always beating on me for everything that was faintly wrong in his "cop eyes." My friends were not getting beat like I was. You could not tell me that such physical punishment was not a form of abuse both physically and emotionally. I was not stupid. I was a teen needing love and guidance, needing understanding and patience with the trauma I was experiencing in my life. This man made me feel completely unloved. To me, he was one cruel man. My mother? Why did she allow this behavior? Did she believe this was how to treat her "baby?" In today's world, I would have the right to call child welfare and they would investigate the home, possibly counsel the parents and the child. They would find out why this child was getting such harsh punishment when the other siblings did not. Once I had been slapped and had a mark on my face. When I went to school, it was noticed but nobody did anything about it. Were they afraid of this man? Today, it is the law to investigate what happened and to counsel parents on their parenting skills. If abuse is found, there are other avenues explored for the safety of all concerned.

Another incident, which has been difficult to put out of my mind was when my mother's husband had come home from work and he discovered that all of my chores had not been completed. I think the main thing was that I had not cleaned the bathroom. He told me to clean the house and get started now. The way he spoke to me made me very angry and whatever I said or did, I know that I was in the kitchen and looking down a .38 caliber gun barrel. The man behind the gun, was looking in my face saying, "Go ahead, move and you will be a ghost in the morning." What was I to think? What was I to do? I froze. My brother was in the living room changing a light bulb. I called out to him. "Andre, he is pointing a gun at me!" My brother thought that this man was just fooling around at first but when he came down from the ladder and saw what was really happening, Andre was also upset. In the time it took Andre to come down from the ladder and come to the kitchen, my mother's husband had lowered the gun and hit me on the cheek bone with the handle of the gun leaving a scar which I still have today. Maybe I should have done the chores more quickly instead of watching television, but I did not deserve this excessive type of punishment. But, sometimes in families, parents are dealing with the stress of their job and the stress of their own impurities which makes them explode. The child's behavior ignites the fuel and "Wham!" Psychological damage was inflicted on me which probably was not meant, but nevertheless occurred. When my mother came home I guess that there was a discussion between them, and the next thing I knew my brother and I went over to my grandmother's house where we stayed for a time. My grandmother was very upset and argued with my mom and step dad telling them that there was no excuse for such actions and reactions. The pain of this man's punishment was not enough. My mother and her husband came over later and took my brother home, but left me there. I felt that my mother cared more about her "man" than she did about her own child, her youngest son. I could not understand it and could not accept it. Once more, I saw Andre as the favored son and I was nothing. I hated my mother at that particular time. Soon, I was going to be "off the hook!".

CHAPTER 2

Troubles

When teens feel unloved and are reaching out for attention, many times they reach for alcohol, drugs, women, sex, or a life of crime. It happens in the twenty first century and it happened in the twentieth century. My way of gaining attention and reacting to life was to involve myself in the drug scene. I fell victim to selling and smoking marijuana. It appeared to me that everyone in the school smoked. I thought this seemed like a way to make some money and before long, I was actually smoking it too, and on a regular basis. I was sure at that time that it was the only way to Survive the Game of My Life.

Now, in order to support a habit of drugs, it takes money. The more you do it, the more intense the desire for stronger drugs. It didn't make much difference where I was, I smoked weed. Whether on the train, at home, or in the car, I thought I had to smoke. Then I started using cocaine. I don't remember exactly who encouraged me to try something stronger, but I think it was a girl with whom I thought I had fallen in love. Love makes you do crazy things sometimes.

Selling weed was not enough to support the habit, so there was this "dude" who coerced me into helping him steal car radios. We went out to the malls on Long Island, and in no more than three seconds the guy could be in and out of a car with the radio in his hand. He wasn't that good that he never got caught because somebody saw the license plate number of the car we were in and contacted the police. Here is where the real trouble began. We were arrested and I got five years probation in addition to a very sore derriere. My parents bailed me out with five hundred dollars, which was much to my amazement but definite relief.

Truly, it is very astonishing to think that I actually graduated from High School. Much credit must be given to the teachers I had and to the man who started the Council for Unity at our school. Council for Unity was and is an organization to help young adults of various cultures to learn how to get along, to try to bring harmony and peace, and to help students learn how to solve problems without violence. I was invited by a girlfriend at that time to attend Council meetings. That support helped me to make it through school because my drug habit continued. However, I managed to apply to a local college, was accepted, and took some great courses in which I did well. The movie theatre hired me to work part time and I was scamming tickets just to support my cocaine habit. That's what it was! A habit! I began to be ruthless about doing things. It became easy to mug people and steal women's pocketbooks since that is something you learn to do when you are out there with the crack heads. Once when working a security job, I locked myself in and helped myself to items I could sell on the street to get what

I needed to survive my drug habit. Then I decided I couldn't continue with college. There was little time now to study. My goals had changed so I withdrew. My mind was messed up with the cocaine.

From high school on, I was living in many different places. Sometimes I was at my mother's house in an apartment where the rooms were quite small but mostly I stayed out roaming the streets or on occasion I would stay with a friend in our neighborhood. My grandmother always had the door open for me and she was just down the street a few blocks. My mother was fed up with my behavior and actually, at one point, I was kicked out of my own home. As a parent now myself, I have a better understanding of how disappointing my behavior must have been to my mother

In 1988 I started smoking crack. A drug addict is definitely of a different mindset, or perhaps it could be said that the addict maintains a self-destruct mode. Nothing really matters to you but to get another hit to take you to that place you were just at in your mind. Sometimes you might be paranoid, thinking that people are watching you. You start looking around, on the floor, out the windows, expecting someone to be after you. You strive to get enough money working to support your habit and when the money runs out from the job, you steal to get what you need. It could be money, jewelry, or whatever you could take from someone without their knowing it. Cocaine is a dangerous drug, locking you up into your own world where nothing matters but you and the "cane" sitting next to you. It is as though it is your best friend when in reality it is your worst nightmare. However, you do not know that at the time you are using the drugs. The drug tells you to do things with the mind working so hard to go get it again. The body becomes so keyed up to have another hit that you must do whatever is necessary for you to get the drug you need. I stole from my family, my friends, my job until I just couldn't do it anymore and I RAN AWAY! I ran into the city and became one of those 42nd Street druggies. That was the place. GET HIGH! GET HIGH! You didn't have to worry about anything. I was too afraid to mess with anything else like meth, dope, and those other types of drugs. Just Cane! I should have been afraid of that. Here I was, living as a homeless person. I was from a decent family and went totally off the deep end. I saw guys and girls of all ages just give up their bodies to get the money to buy the drugs to support their unending habit. The top dealers in the city would come down by the boxes where they knew the drug addicts were hanging out. They would pick out workers and put them on 42nd and Eighth or Ninth Avenue. They would put YOU out there so that they were not in the shot gun way, meaning that they might escape arrest. There are all types of games to get the drugs. You can call the police on yourself and if the drug boss is standing there beside you, he will walk off and you have his package. It doesn't matter to you. You are going to get high regardless. You are not thinking about any consequences. You are not thinking that your life could be over because you robbed the man's drugs. I was the top seller on 42nd Street at that time. Everybody liked to get me to sell their drugs because I knew all the crack heads and they all knew I wasn't selling it unless it was the best around. They would come to me and I was making lots of money but was smoking it as fast as I made it. I smoked anywhere I felt like smoking. I smoked in a crack in the wall or a phone booth. You feel like superman and look at a girl and are bonked out.

I was living in a box at 40th and Eighth Avenue, a place known as Honeycomb Hideout. I spent about a year there. One winter I recall moving the boxes over the grates above the subway; heat would rise up through the grates and provide some warmth. Sometimes we would hang out at the Port Authority and sleep on the stairwells at night until the police would have us move in the morning. On days when it would rain or snow, we would get plastic from garbage cans and cover the boxes to keep them dry. Another way to keep warm was to stuff newspapers down in your clothing as a type of insulation. The inside of the large boxes was like a little studio apartment. Clothes were kept inside there and usually a stash of snacks. Everyone would go to Honeycomb Hideout because they knew it was the best place to get high in the city. Police didn't bother much with you there. Just occasionally they might come and check out what was happening. Once I got arrested over there for having paraphernalia, but it wasn't anything. They let me back out on the street. Later, I was caught for a direct sale. This then was a felony. Now, I was booked and my family had to be called to be told that I was arrested. They were naturally upset and concerned. I recall that they had a family meeting to discuss what was happening to me. I didn't care much because they had turned their backs on me previously and I was HIGH on the drugs.

JAIL! JAIL! Jail is not a place that I had ever been before and it sure was not the best place to survive living. Jail is not a place of luxury. The atmosphere is one of no rights and you feel

less than a human being and truly, most inmates have been living like animals. The authorities in the jail try to shock you into
being a productive citizen so that you do not want to be there
again even though more than 50% are repeat offenders.

The first place I was incarcerated was a Detention Center.
I was about 18 at the time. It was necessary to be in a program
to detoxify me. I was scared for a minute. Living in jail, I had
a correction officer coming to tell me what time to eat, what
time to exercise, what time to do anything outside my room.
This place was clean. There was a door that locked whenever
I had to go in or out. There was one bunk in the room, and the
phones were outside the room with a television in the day-
room. Most centers and jails have similar organization and
programs.

There was plenty of time to think about what I had done
and where I should be going. I felt like a caged animal. As I
thought about what had led me to this place, thought about my
family, thought about the kind of person I was, I truly wanted to
change. In jail, you no longer have a name. You have a number
by which you must live, and you address the officers as though
they are royalty. I never knew much about jail but I sure got a
crash course very quickly. People get raped in jail; get cut, and
yes, even robbed. It happened frequently. The way I decided to
cope was to stick to myself and take care of me. The only time
people get into a confrontation is if the other inmates think
you are too soft and they try to take advantage of you. If they
think you are too hard, they will want to make an example of
you. The too hard characters may try to extort you and get your
food from the commissary, telling you to have your people

drop such and such in your account. I never had this happen to me as I seemed able to make people understand that I am not a push over. I did not look like a mean guy because I had a good looking face but a mean attitude. So there really were not any major problems for me while locked up. However, I really wanted more from life than living in jail, killing time, wasting my life. If you have no life, it probably wouldn't matter as much to you because you have food, a place to lay your head, and you have sports or other activities in which to participate. There are inmates who would rather commit a crime and be back in jail rather than living in a box or under a bridge. For me, my idea was to do this time, get my physical and mental self together, and move on.

Once you have a felony record, if you get another charge you get more jail time than you had before. My program of detoxification must not have been long enough or as intense as I needed to make me want to stay away from the place I had been. Strong support is needed and if you don't have it, the likelihood of going back to jail is close to one hundred percent. Society does not help you, you must help yourself. So, like a fool, I decided to put myself to the test and I went back to the same place I had been, stood around those smokers, walked around and found out I really was not strong enough. I did not have the support needed at that time and I fell victim to the drug scene again. It took only a few days and I looked like I had never left the corner. In jail, I had good food, ate well, and gained weight, but on the corner, once you are on that cocaine, you don't want to eat. If you eat one meal in two or three days, that is too much. So I was back into oblivion. I actually thought about death. I wanted to die but smoking that cocaine makes your eyes open up wide into a never-ending room where you hear different sounds and voices. I recall walking eight or nine days straight without eating or sleeping. It didn't matter to an individual so high on drugs. After this type of behavior, I'd sleep for two or three days. This was allowed to happen. Nobody bothered me, nobody took me away, and there were many others doing the same thing.

One night, I was out there and heard a voice that I didn't expect to hear. I had just come out of a store where I had picked up some things, was ready to go get a hit, and around the corner, there was my man, my partner, my best friend, my everlasting soul brother. We had grown up together, same neighborhood from the time we were about five or six years old. This young man had grown up across the street from my grandparents. When we were teens, and later young adults, we enjoyed going to amusement parks together, especially to Coney Island. As video games became popular, we shared an enthusiasm for that entertainment. My bond with this friend was tighter than with the other guys in the neighborhood. When it was rough at my house, if I didn't go to my grandmother, I went to stay at my soul brother's home. I was always welcome there. I stood there as he came near and heard him say that I was not to run. I didn't think I ever ran from anything, but in reality I know today that I was running from all that would make me strong. He talked to me until I cried. He said, "Damon, please, please come to the shop tomorrow and we will work this out." I knew how he wanted me to answer and I said, "I am going to be there." As you might guess,

I never made it. As he walked away, I cried and smoked the rest of the drugs I had until there was no more. If he had insisted on taking me with him right then and there, would I have gone? Why didn't he take me then? The answer I know is that he trusted me as his soul brother and truly thought that I would come the next day. He didn't realize what those drugs had been doing to me. A few days later, I ran into one of the Dominican bosses and he asked me if I wanted to work. I was ready to do that. I remember the morning very well as it was the last I was to see the streets for a long time. Bright and early, one of the only hustlers to be out there, a white man came onto me and I knew he was a policeman. I didn't care! About five minutes after he bought from me, I got rushed and was arrested. This was another felony so I knew there were no games to be played with me. I was not coming home anytime soon. I was smoked out and looked really bad, with messed up hair, bad odor, and the same clothes on my body that I had been wearing for about four or five weeks. It didn't matter to me then!!!!

This felony was indeed handled differently, because I had a record. I had been placed in a "holding type" facility where I had to await sentencing. In the meantime, once more the detoxification was started; the many meetings which are similar to Alcoholics Anonymous were mandatory and continued throughout the entire incarceration. When I had phone privileges, my family did not want to accept the collect calls, and they did not come to see me. My friend from the old neighborhood came a lot. He put money in my account and brought his wife and kids to see me and this meant a lot to me. In that year I started cutting hair at the barber shop within the facility. I found that I was quite good at doing that and my friend suggested that when I came home, I could work with him at his dad's barber shop business. That sounded like a true blessing to me and it gave me a goal to work toward. Actually, I developed a lot of skill cutting hair while I was there.

As I sat in this facility, there was much time to think and I knew that there was going to be a lot more time before I would be sentenced. Before going to trial, the jury had to be picked. Before the jury is picked, you are placed in a room with the judge, the District Attorney, and the lawyer and you talk for the last time. The judge indicated that if I chose to go to trial with a jury, I would likely get twelve and a half to twenty five years in jail. In my mind, everything went blank. All they caught me with was three vials of crack. I could not understand such a stiff penalty for having so little on my person when caught. I looked at my lawyer and asked him if we could beat this and he said that we had a 50/50 chance. He was a legal aid lawyer. When the judge next spoke, he said I could take two and a half and get out of his court room or go to trial and he would give me the maximum. I was no fool and decided that the best thing to do was to take the lesser of the sentences offered. It wouldn't take a rocket scientist to decide what made the most sense, but this incarceration would be upstate.

What kind of life had I chosen? What had I allowed myself to become? Could I get a stronger ego now and move on with my life? Could I find the real ME and learn how to survive the game of life in a more acceptable mode? Did I want to improve myself, be proud of me and make my family proud of me instead of thinking I had become the so-called "black sheep" of the family? Why was I continually choosing self destruction? How did I feel about me? Did I have respect for myself?

It was easy to determine in my mind, very early in this next incarceration, that this kind of life was not what I truly wanted for myself. Doing time upstate and in other types of facilities soon made an impression upon me. I had said this before but made the wrong choices over and over. This was not what I would be doing again. At the holding section of the next correctional institution, they shaved my head and sprayed me down with some type of bug spray. This is what they did! I didn't believe this was for real when I saw it on television shows but it proved to be true. They spray your naked body with a spray to "cleanse" whatever you might have on yourself. I guessed that it was supposed to change people somehow too, because it was a humiliating and very degrading feeling. The next step was to transfer me to a Shock facility which was run like a six month boot camp. Hard discipline was executed where you decide you will do this time or take the consequences. This part was not difficult for me from the mere fact that it was doing something meaningful and was physically good for me as well as mentally stimulating. All of this discipline training of my body and mind was to make this thing that I was going though a lot easier. It was at this place and with this training, that my determination to live a more productive life when released from prison grew to outstanding proportions. The authorities made me a flag carrier, which was a high honor there, leading the class, running in front of the platoon singing the cadence and leading the class through the physical training, jogging, etc. They had us up at five in the morning to start our work-out program. All through the day, there was a schedule to keep you moving in the right direction. A red flag went up one day when I was told that my blood pressure was too high to keep me in this place and that it had not stabilized as they had hoped. This meant that once more I would be transferred, leave this program where I felt I was doing so well, and enter a minimum security facility where they would emphasize the ASAT program.

An ASAT program is much like an Alcoholics Anonymous program. You feel like you are being brainwashed with monotonous statements they expect you to believe and accept. Being a man who had far more intelligence than I ever used in school and after graduation, some days were tough. I had to reach inside of me and use what I had learned so far to become the CHAMPION of my life, the SURVIVOR of just another part of life. I continued to train physically, and was lifting six hundred twenty five pounds about ten times each in the squats. On my chest, I was doing about three hundred pounds. I lifted about one hundred pounds or more with my arms. I attended school and did a lot of programming, trying to talk about what I was going to do later in my journey of life.

Jail gives you lots of time to think and try to understand yourself. It gives you time to open up to many avenues and to try to find the right way to go. You might be intelligent and know what you need to do, but some people cannot change. They revert back to the old lifestyle. This was what I had done up until now. Quite frankly, there are many others who come out into society and have no way to continue but down the self destruct path. They cannot face their families and be out on the streets. Soon they are back in jail, their home for most of their youth and adult life. This was not going to be me. I meditated many days and nights about the experiences I had and would have until I was released. Making sense out of life is truly a mind game, but that is what you go through. The ultimate mind game! Beating myself mentally everyday, promising myself that I could and would do better. There are older inmates, life criminals, who tend to be mentors. They rotate in and out of the penitentiaries. Well, there was one who mentored me on how to survive this jail time. He encouraged learning and writing. He was primarily concerned with having me know that I could survive with a support system and stay out of jail for good. While there, I had to do the time and not let the time do me.

During this long stay in prison, my mother began to communicate with me through letters. She would send me money when she could, but often she had little to spare. I got some tattoos while I was in jail and one had my mother and sister's name on my chest. I felt that if anything, I would always have them a part of me because no matter what had happened in my past, I could not stop loving my mother. The love of a mother just never changes. My sister! My sister was there for me sometimes, even though I had stolen from her. She tried to give me support, gave me some money or what I might need, and would accept phone calls when possible. Truly it would not have surprised me if she would have been unwilling to help me or forgive me. But she never let me forget what I had done.

Another experience while incarcerated was attending school to get my reading and math to a better level. The teacher I had for these classes was a Caucasian lady who had recently divorced her husband. She had such a brain in her head that I knew that I would learn a lot and I wanted to put forth the best effort I could. She seemed to know her students so very well.

She knew who to spend the most time with and if they were serious about learning. Some of the guys in the class were definitely not there to learn but to pass the time of day and make it look good on the reports sent to their files. She seemed impressed with my ability to verbalize many concepts and gave me great suggestions about doing the homework which she expected us to do. I was very happy with the encouragement this lady gave me. I saw her as a very strong person with a glow about her teaching and a sincerity with which she spoke. Back in the dorm, I spent a lot of time wondering if this woman could be my support when I would be out of prison. Would she want to do that? What was she planning to do with her life? One thing was certain, and that was that I could not speak much to her about anything personal. However, one day she informed me that she was resigning from her position in corrections as she realized that she was prone to be an enabler. Her Christian teaching and her life of doing for others was putting her in a position which could be a problem for her in the prison teaching program. I told her that I needed to talk to her as I would like her to be of support to me as I finished my time and got on a work release program. She seemed to feel that would not be a problem when she took another job. So, I had her name put on my visitation list. The authorities would not come after me for being friendly with a former teacher. I had played it real cool. I could not have her visit me when she worked for the prison school. That was definitely a no-no. After she left and came to visit me, some of the officers looked at me as if to say, "How did you manage to do that?" There tends to be a lot of prejudice inside the penitentiary and because I was a Panamanian with light brown skin and this woman was white, this was certainly not acceptable. Many of the officers really liked me and they didn't truly care because they saw that I had my head right and was determined to have my own support system when I was out in society. They expressed that they knew I would not be one to return to the system.

This woman became a truer friend than I had known among all the females in my life. She had strong feelings about the way the Corrections department was run and that there was little done to keep inmates from returning to the system. So my asking if she would help me and be my support system was something she could not refuse because she was on a mission to prove to the state authorities that there was a better way to handle those who were ready to rejoin society.

CHAPTER 3

Making Choices

The period of life where I had many hours to think and to get my head right involved another brief transfer and then a work release program. Freedom! Wow! What a feeling after years living with criminals, away from family and friends, and limited communication with anyone on the outside. Few family members ever bothered with me. And phone calls? Forget it. All calls had to be collect calls and seldom did anyone accept the calls. Each day while imprisoned, I would hope someone might pick up the phone and accept the call but each day I was disappointed. This was just another instance of surviving this game of life and feeling that nobody really cared about me.

Coming back into the old neighborhood where I grew up was somewhat tough to do. It seemed like the crew there had stepped up their drug game. It was so easy to get back into selling but also surprising to me that a person who had been so strung out on drugs was now bagging half a kilo of cocaine and not affected in any way. It was only a thirst for the almighty dollar. My crew was into transporting drugs into the south where you could get a high dollar amount for miniscule portions of the drugs. Along with having such large amounts of drugs you need a large arsenal as protection. We found ourselves venturing into other forms of getting money. We had these weapons, so we should use them. We had a contact who knew when large shipments of marijuana and cocaine would be arriving into the states. Like an elite strike force, my team would go to work with scanners in hand, cars full of weapons, duct tape, and hand cuffs and proceed as if it was a regular job. Sometimes it would take a day or as long as a week, to seize the right opportunity for my team to go to work. I was a driver and knew the roads like the back of my hand. For those desiring a quick get away, it was my car to hop into and feel secure.

One job that we were sent on involved a three hundred pound shipment of marijuana. My team was eager to move. There was no going home without this weed. Everybody jumped in about three cars. The first job was to secure the residence. We did it with such precision and in broad daylight. The house was captured and the people were made immobile but very much alive. At this point, the owners of the shipment came and we were already inside. They were ordered to show us where the stash was located. They had no choice but to co-operate. Before long, it was in my apartment. After selling this shipment, we rewarded ourselves with the purchase of Suzuki Dirt Bikes. A couple of the guys knew how to ride and others were novices. But, I had been riding a long time. Motorcycles were fun for popping wheelies and picking up girls. Those were the fun times with the bike but little did I know that my fun times would abruptly be halted down the road of time.

After a while, the crew began to feel a lot of heat so we decided to separate and each go to a separate state. It was our intention to throw the authorities off our trail. I went south because I had family there and was already established, not realizing that this would be the biggest move in my hustling career. Before long, with all my hustling skills, I reached the level of Kingpin. I recall taking a flight back home with over twenty five thousand dollars in cash. Mine! All mine! I was so excited because now I could buy one kilo of cocaine. Was that what I really wanted to do? Should I really stay with this style of life?

How to organize my life and stay straight was going to be a challenge, but I had promised myself that I never again would be an inmate in a penal institution. Living with my sister was necessary for a few months while on work release. Her apartment was small and she was living there with her young son. Conditions were crowded but this was not going to be permanent. This was not the best arrangement. I was in a quandary as to how to survive "out here" and to be back in the old neighborhood was not ideal. The old crew was there with all the temptation in the world in front of me. Yes, there I was, back in the "hood." There were things I needed or wanted and it was necessary, or so I thought, to make the quick money by selling drugs but not using them. I was taking many risks but I had learned how to avoid the police. It was also a risk that I could be shot by other drug dealers. This went on for a short period of time as I tried to get myself on the right track and money in my pocket.

Finding a job was important. The movie theater had been a haven at one time, and again I was there. I had to follow work release rules and check in with the authorities and they checked on me periodically. My mainstay was with my dear best friend and his dad at the barber shop. The training I had had at the detention center was going to pay off. I enrolled in a Barber School in Manhattan, and that learning experience helped me gain the skill to cut many heads of hair. There were techniques which were taught there such as how to lay hair down without taking a fade too high. Learning about the grains of hair, and understanding the circles of hair on the head, was essential to knowing the right way to give a haircut. Working in a reputable shop was important as the pay is great and the hours long. It became quite natural for me to cut hair and gain a clientele which would return week after week.

My teacher friend moved to Queens when she was able to find a job with the New York City schools. She lived for a few years in my cousin's basement apartment and encouraged me to work full time at the barber shop. This was a very busy shop and I loved styling hair. Working twelve hour days from Wednesday through Sunday was quite usual. Many people became regular customers and liked the designs I could cut into their hair if they desired to have it done. Back then it was very popular in the "hood."

My barber shop partner and best friend introduced me to many people. He and I were known as womanizers and neither of us was bad looking. Women were frequently attracted to us. We had lots of conversations on how to capitalize on this characteristic of ourselves. In the meantime, I was driving a white convertible. Wherever I went, girls would flock around the car and want to talk and get a ride. It seemed that the girls thought I was quite the catch. You would have thought that I was LL Cool J. This one day a jeep drove up beside me and all these girls were flirting with me, wanting their pictures taken with me. There was one who was dark skinned who wanted to know which of the girls I liked best. She was an exotic dancer and had been having a lot of shows. She and I became attracted to one another and I took her to all her strip shows. My barber shop buddy and I then joined in a cooperative venture with her to hire exotic dancers and hold dances much like a strip club. We generated a lot of money from these dance clubs and of course, got to know many different types of women. There was never a time that I was involved sexually with the dancers who we hired, just the woman business partner who had two children, a boy and a girl. The boy knew his father but the girl did not and so she adopted me as her father. We continue that contact to this day. At the same time that I had this association with her mother, there were many other women on the side.

Women! I had my share of women of various cultures and nationalities. I could drive around the old neighborhood and stop every few yards as there would be someone who knew me and wanted to talk, glad to see me out there. But, it was the women I met who always were infatuated with me. I have been blessed or maybe some would say cursed, with a way to charm the women. Women do not even have to be beautiful for me to talk in such a way that they think I am madly in love with them. It has been quite usual to date a different woman every night, have lunch or dinner with someone else, and on and on.

Enjoying women, charming women is one thing, but I have had some one night affairs where nine months later, the woman is calling and saying she has had a baby and that I am the father. The first woman who did this had declared that the father could not be anybody else but me. She had given birth to a girl who was named for my mother. Over the years, I realized she had been seeing other men and I began to wonder about the validity of her claim. Then she wanted child support and the court ordered DNA testing which proved it was nearly one hundred percent positive I was NOT the father. My life was becoming like a Maury Povich television show. Another woman met me at a club and she was always staring at me as I danced to the extreme. My friend Frankie was there and she went up to him, spoke to him, and he gave her my phone number. We met later. She had actually been living with someone and I was seeing someone I had thought I might want to marry someday. She later claimed I was the father of her son and he became my namesake. Still another year after that, a boy was born to a woman for whom I had very strong feelings and he carried my middle and last name. None of the mothers of the children who bore my family name knew about the others. They thought that their child was the only child I had fathered.

I had never thought much about becoming a father. I was not brought up to have a child out of wedlock, and my life was not conducive to being a responsible father. I needed to get myself straight. However, as I began thinking about what it would be like to be a father, I thought a lot about not having my own dad and living with my mother's husband. I realized that I did not have a role model. All I could do was try to be what I had wished for in my own life.

The last child whose mother I enjoyed and maybe loved was positive I was her child's father and so was I. He bore such a resemblance to me. He and I became quite attached to each other. I found fatherhood to be rather scary, but this little tiger was contented with my feeding him and putting him to rest for the night. Once he was asleep, I frequently would leave and be about my business, hanging with friends or whatever the mood dictated.

CHAPTER 4

Life Changing Experience

The next phase of my life was nothing I could have predicted or imagined was ever going to happen. The year was 1997. It was early in April when we had celebrated my younger son's first birthday. Now the date was April 30th. That morning I arose and prepared to attend a volunteer activity sponsored by the Council for Unity, the organization which had been started at my high school. The friends and acquaintances I had made in this group did not know all that I had been going through, but knew me as a good man. In this organization, you promise to be the best you can be and try to have all nationalities come together and help one another. These people knew me as the hair stylist who was doing extremely well with his life NOW. It was not unusual for me to volunteer to speak to young people in the schools or to drop everything and go when the Council organizer or one of the officers would call and ask me to serve on a panel. I was telling these students how not to live because I had been down the road of eluding police and cheating life and death. I had been one of those youths who had owned many guns but now could tell them not to pick up guns. I had been one of those youths who did not study but now could tell them to study and be the best people they could be. Meanwhile, inside my mind, I knew that I had frequently done the opposite. There is a saying I believe, that is, "do as I say and don't do as I did." Perhaps this was a way for me to heal and give back to the community what I had taken. When I was the age of these young people, nobody was giving me that advice, or maybe I didn't want to hear it. As teens and young adults, sometimes we think we are invincible. We think that we know everything when in fact we know very little about life. It all happened so fast.

April 30th was a bright and sunny day. I had decided to ride my motorcycle to the Council meeting as a few days previously I had a slight accident with the car and the hood had a dent. Being a "fly guy," I was not going to drive my car with a dented hood. NO. I was "Too Cool!" "Too Fly!" I saw some of the guys that day who loved my motorcycle and took pictures of me doing wheelies. Then, I checked in with a partner who also took a picture or two of me, and finally I went to the meeting. After the meeting at the school with a rather difficult group (Council had been called in because of gang violence) we all decided to go to a restaurant to eat and discuss what we had been doing and how we could improve future presentations. I had to leave early to pick up my youngest son's mother from the college she was attending in Manhattan. I left the restaurant and got on my motorcycle, heading toward the stoplight. Since I had to be who I was, I jumped up on the seat of my motorcycle and did a grandstand. As I approached the light, I saw a jeep come out from somewhere, headed right toward me. Since I was in a grandstand, I knew that I couldn't bring the bike down fast enough. I watched the driver's face from the time she came out until she hit me. She didn't look once to the right to see if anything was coming as she made a U-turn at this five-street intersection. After the contact with the bike, I don't remember what happened next.

When I opened my eyes in the ambulance, one of my friends from Council for Unity was sitting next to me telling me that everything was going to be alright. I was strapped down in an effort to keep me stable and unable to make any moves. Many people at the scene thought I was dead. Be alright? For some reason, I knew that was not going to be the case. I could not feel my legs. They had me in a head brace so I could not move my neck. No, this was not looking good. They had taken me to the hospital on Staten Island as this was the hospital in the area on call for trauma accidents. When I got there, I was concentrating on trying to move my legs. I couldn't feel anything. I could move my arms but they had me strapped in so I really couldn't move them either. I didn't feel any pain. Nothing! The next thing I knew, they were rushing me to surgery to stabilize my neck. When I came out of surgery, I was in the hallway, waiting to go to ICU. I recall hearing a doctor talking to somebody, telling them that I had broken my neck. Would I truly survive was discussed by all who stood by. In my life, I had heard that people die when they have a broken neck. That was the only thing I ever knew. With a broken neck, you die!! Later, I came to realize that I had broken my neck in two places and I was still alive. The level of my spinal injury was called a C-7, C-6 and I had broken my hip too. This day would change my life forever. This was more than most people could believe or accept, yet

I was still living. To think of all that I had been through in my life, and now to be paralyzed! Was this how the divine power wakes you up to think about how tenuous life really is? Why didn't I die? The answer to that question was to be answered many years down the road of my life. When the doctor came in to my bedside, he did explain to me that I had broken my neck in two places, and that I had broken my hip. They had placed eighty-four stitches from the hip down and the doctor's prognosis was that I would never walk again. Being the person I had been, I really couldn't believe what this man had just said. Actually, I never truly accepted the fact that he thought I would not walk again. All that I knew then was that I was paralyzed and wondered what it would take to SURVIVE THE GAME OF LIFE. Two seconds earlier or two seconds later, if I had stayed in the restaurant, if I had chosen to be seated on my bike, if, if, if. Would I still be able to walk? Timing would have been different! You just never know for sure. You play out the cards that have been dealt to you if you are strong enough to do so. Yes, this was going to be a true test of strength and endurance, a test of perseverance and of faith.

The emotions and the mental state of a person who has had such trauma are key to recovery, along with a strong support system. I had experienced these needs earlier in my life but apparently had not learned enough about myself. Life tends to be taken for granted when we are young and I can definitely say that was true for me. Party, have fun, take chances. That had been central in my life for so many years. At this point, after the first surgery, I just did not think I could tackle the tough job of recovery. To see myself being paralyzed for the rest of my life was just an unbelievable thought. Who did I know in this situation? Nobody!! There were many days and nights in which my foremost concern was how I could commit suicide in this place and end it all. There was not a single person who I could convince to bring me a gun. I had told my teacher/friend to bring one saying I would use it and she would not have to worry about anything. She was too smart for that line. My mother's husband recalls that I had told him to do the same thing, and there was no way he was going to sit in jail for helping me end my life. They all wanted me to live. During the week after the neck surgery, I went into crisis as I had an infection in one of the incisions in my neck. My fever was upwards of 106 and 107, and I was going in and out of consciousness. There are sketchy scenes in my memory of those first few weeks but I do know that many family members were there, my teacher friend was there, Council for Unity members came frequently, and there were many of my women friends there, including the mothers of the children who claimed me as the father. I had been living a hell of a life which was about to reach new heights in a far different way than I had ever anticipated. My mother and teacher companion/support stood by me with family and friends often in a chain of bowed heads. I could feel the presence but do not recall all the faces every time they were there.

I thought this hospital was trying to kill me! I would lie in the bed, the room was dark, and I would call out and nobody would come to me. However, this intensive care room was located right next to the nurses' station. Probably because I was in and out of consciousness, I didn't realize how much time people did attend to me. I started having extreme nightmares and began to feel paranoid. My teacher, who was and is truly the best friend anyone could desire or expect to have, stayed at the hospital day and night for nearly a week or more and was the advocate for me throughout my hospital stay. After she had to go back to work she would come directly from school in the afternoon, leave the latest that she could, and was there every weekend. This woman never wavered from her mission to get me home and to have the best care possible.

When my mother arrived, she stayed at night with me. There were complaints from some of the other patient families in ICU, but she was only able to be up from Florida for a few weeks and my condition was critical for those same weeks. When she first saw me, she saw her youngest child with tubes coming out of every hole where they could put something to keep me stabilized. In fact, one night the doctors told my mother that I might not make it until morning. How could my mother deal with this? This was the son who was the dancer, the outspoken child whose behavior she had not always approved of, the son who was not pleased with his mother's choices. But, this was her blood! She had given birth to me and loved me with a heartfelt love. She stood at my bedside and prayed with me and kept encouraging me to keep fighting and not give up the gift of life. Her words were, "You can't leave me, Damon. We are fighters. You cannot give up!" Those words were to ring in my ears many times just as they are recalled now.

Being paralyzed was something I did not know much about but surely had to learn and understand. I knew a few people who were in wheelchairs but not many and I never paid much attention to them or to how they felt about their situations. I was too busy living the life, being the man, being the Kingpin of the area. There was nothing else that needed to be done because I was the man. Nothing else needed to happen but what was going on. So now reality slaps me, and jerks me to a halt. I had been moving a thousand miles per hour and suddenly a brick wall just stopped me. No movement! Oh, this is not the life for me! Let me put an end to this right now. They won't bring me a gun so let's see what other way is possible. I pulled the IV out of my arm, allowing the blood to squirt out of the vein. I lay there watching the blood squirt in various directions, splattering red all around me on the sheets and over my arm and at the same time asking myself if I really wanted to die. In many ways, the answer was yes, but in other instances, the answer was no. The greatest fear I had was the pain I knew my people would have in my passing. At the same time, I truly didn't care. It seemed this was an out for me. Forget my kids, forget my mother, my family, my true friend and advocate. Why should I live? The nurses eventually came and caught me, strapped me up, and put the IV back in my arm in such a way that I could not take it out again.

For days and days, I lay in that bed. There were metal pieces screwed into my head, supports to keep me from moving my neck. My legs were elevated and braced to keep me from making the slightest move. Therefore, is it any wonder that I could not eat, did not desire food, and started to lose a lot of weight? Then, a pressure sore developed on the back of my left foot because they had put a type of boot on my foot which did not allow it to breathe. My friend nearly had a stroke when she peeked in the boot and found the skin on my heels had turned black. She made quite a fuss and demanded attention be given to this condition immediately. The doctor changed the orders and began treating the problem. I also had a pressure sore on my butt due to the fact that I could not be turned. Later, that sore healed when they were able to start moving me.

There had been five surgeries in about five weeks. The sixth surgery was a tracheotomy which left a horrible scar in the front of me. I was so vain before this accident! It doesn't seem possible that someone could have been so conceited. I always had a certain faith but truly did not bring the great POWER into my life until this accident gave me so much time to think about living and dying. It seemed like this Power was speaking some cold hard truths to help make me a different person, to see things in a different light. That Power was saying to me that I was not being taken off this earth because He had a reason to keep me here. I heard this voice say, "Damon, I am going to allow you to see certain things, MY SON, so that you can understand who I am and who you should be. You must come to respect everything that you are and respect the people around you. You must respect to the fullest degree. I am not going to take you from this earth now because you have work to do on earth. You have work to do for ME. You have work to do for yourself but, I have taken everything that you thought was important so that you truly live the life that was meant for you to live." Well, many times my grandmother would say that in life the Lord does not give us more than we can handle. You know what? Damn! HE has put so many burdens on my shoulders now and I have no choice but to choose to do what He has directed me to do.

Being faced with this horrible, very visible scar on my neck is something of which I have been so ashamed. I can't really do anything about it. Vitamin E is supposed to be helpful in the healing process of the scar and make it less noticeable. Perhaps over time that will occur. The biggest psychological problem with this scar is that doctors in the rehab hospital said it was not really a necessary surgery. This has been hard to push aside mentally. Also, I faced the fact that I had no use of my legs. I lost the use of my bodily functions, too. Yes, I am able to sustain an erection, but I can't feel like I felt before the accident. Then, I lost over eighty percent of the use of my hands but I knew that physical therapy was planned for that to improve. Paralyzed from my upper chest down, there was no feeling on the outside but there have been some feelings on the inside which is strange and hard to explain. One of the other body functions I lost involved the elimination of waste products, both solid and liquid. I could not always do my own bowel movement manually as my hands did not have the ability to make the right movements to force it out. Thus, adaptive measures have had to be instituted which are not always pleasant. In time, as my hands became somewhat better able to manipulate the right movements, I have been able to do it without adaptive steps. I have a leg bag connected with tubing and condom over my penis. If the flow is a certain way, if the tubing or condom gets twisted, I urinate all over myself. On a few occasions, I have had the solid waste come down when I was in places that it was so embarrassing. How I used to be is gone. What is going to change? Anything? I have questioned over and over again as I have wondered if I have the strength to accept the new person I must be.

Those early years of
innocence.

True friendship is hard to find. (Frankie and D)

Outdoor life keeps you healthy.

Happy, proud mother keeps on smiling

Lady with never-ending love

If I had a twin, this is who she'd be. (Tanya)

Love of a child can keep
the heart strong.

Made it to the end of
NYC Marathon.

Miniature golf with dad.

Brothers through thick and thin. (Andre and D)

Coach "Daddy" with his "Mets"

Hope and Possibility
Race in Central Park
— Always a challenge!

Softball life also keeps
you active.

Breakfast is ready!

Happy with "mike" in hand.

Friends for life

Comedy life

Damon Rozier
Photos by JP Justice
tel 917 440 7395

Laughter is the key to
life so I will always keep
laughing.

CHAPTER 5

Horrific Challenges

When it was thought that I was strong enough, the doctor said that it would be best for me to go to another hospital which would have a large rehabilitation unit. There were two possible hospitals in the area and the one which had a bed first was Mt. Sinai Hospital in Manhattan. I was so glad to leave the first hospital and wished that I never had gone there, but then maybe I would have felt that way no matter where I had been a patient with this horrific challenge. However, the transfer was the best thing for me. Placed in a private room, I had therapists who were a team. There was one who has always stuck out in my mind as she made me work and just never gave up on me. She recalls that I was extremely depressed and resisted therapy. I was described as very obstinate on many days when she would enter my room and indicate I had to go for physical therapy. I told her "NO" so many times that it is a wonder that she kept coming back. But, that is what made her so special: her dedication to her responsibility as a therapist. I did not want to exert the energy and could not imagine that all the effort was going to pay dividends. Her first attempt was to just give me a tour of the therapy room and places I would go each day and what they would attempt to do with me. Then daily, she would come to the room and tell me it was time to go and get busy. I was so negative. It did not seem possible to me that I would ever make enough progress to be independent. I could not imagine that I would ever be able to do anything for myself. The nurses and this special therapist would often just talk to me and explain that I had to get my head right and that all the rest would be so much easier. Psychologists, psychiatrists, medical doctors today, tell us that much illness is controlled by the mind. Like in most things in life, we have the good days and the bad days and it seemed at first that I had more bad days than good days. However, as I was able to learn how to get from the bed to the wheelchair, I slowly gained some confidence. The real credit will always be to my therapist who gave me inspiration to dig for the inner strength and desire to get better. She said she could not see me as somebody who was willing to just lie there in the hospital bed and accept myself as being weak. She kept telling me that I must not give up but had to get busy doing what was right and good for me. Her task was not easy but she saw potential for me to do well. The people in this rehab unit continually were supportive of me and sometimes even pulled me out of the bed, expressing every day that nothing was impossible if I would get my mind right. Getting the right motivation was very hard. It was truly rough!!

Then there were some conversations with a psychologist. Maybe the one was truly a psychiatrist. He made it very tough for me mentally as I thought his questions were so insane. He must have believed my head was injured as his questions were,

"Can you tell me your name? Do you know the names of your family members? How old will you be on your birthday?" This line of questioning made me so upset. Day after day, it was the same line of questioning. My therapist assured me that nobody believed me to be crazy and those sessions would not be continued. My teacher/advocate remembers having a conference with the social worker and psychologist also; pleading with them to work on the positive which could be initiated there rather than focusing on what was obviously not a problem. My head was not injured and the focus of mental therapy needed to be on acceptance of my quadriplegic state and how to utilize what I could do.

Being paralyzed, I had no control over the muscles from my upper chest down and so sitting up was difficult. I still have some control issues but have learned how to deal with them. Lying down for such a long period of time, the body reacts to being in that position. The blood rushes to your feet and does not have time to get back to your head so that you feel faint or lightheaded. This was not easy to accept either, because I was always on the go, running here and there and now I had trouble just sitting up and had to tell myself that this was necessary if I was ever going to get out of this hospital. So, my determination to succeed developed as I saw that I could do more each week. It was baby steps in the continuum of the physical therapy program but I could not let this beat me. Progress could continually be made each day with the right attitude.

There was one good thing I remembered about this hospital stay that made me know life was still worth living. The nurse came in to give me a sponge bath and when she started washing me up, there was true elation. I saw I had an erection! Wow!

Could this really be? I truly had not lost all my manhood. Normally family came to visit around 7 pm. This day, around 5 pm, one of my ex-girlfriends entered the room. Now this would be the true test. She couldn't believe my sponge bath story, so she started playing with me and sure enough, it rose right up. Before long, since she was wearing a dress, she removed her panties and got on top of me. Even though the feeling was not the same, just the knowledge that I could please and be pleased made life seem a tad brighter

There were many control issues with which I had to deal and decisions which had to be made. There was a mental and emotional bond that developed with the therapy team in the hospital. As I grew stronger, I knew that I would soon go home. These people gave me the mental tools to believe that it would be OK. They made me know that I would come back there for outpatient therapy and that I would continue to have their support. This was so vital in the long term program which was planned to take place when I would leave the rehabilitation hospital.

Oh yes, there would still be hurdles to surmount. My youngest son's mother thought that she had my only child but like the rest of the women, they all met in the hospital and now there were no more secrets. So, I was about to face a decision that she had made and had told my cousin and uncle long before I knew what was coming. She told them that there was no way she would remain with me and that the relationship was going to end. They begged her to wait until I was stronger and closer to going home to tell me. Now, even though I had cheated on her, I really did care and did not want to lose her but I had deluded myself to believe that what I was doing was right because

I had treated her well when we were together. We had gone many places, had great dinners and I had lavished her with a nice apartment and gifts. Choices! I was so blind. Respect! I did not show respect to anyone including myself. All the things of the world mean nothing if you do not have the right things in your heart and it became apparent that I did not. I had even made her think that I was coming home to her and to our son but I had already made arrangements to go to Queens with my teacher-advocate and friend. That apartment was larger and the drive of this woman as an individual was something I believed in and felt would work for me. She (the teacher) had such an inner drive and faced each day as though she had been placed on this earth with a mission to accomplish and that indeed was just what she planned. She would prove to the world that people need support systems when in any kind of difficulty. We need someone to care and to do what is right to correct a wrong. There was not going to be any failure or obstacle too large for her to tackle and get to the goal. What I needed most of all was to have someone to support me and be attentive to my needs.

As a young man, there was little in life which I had feared. Since the accident, fear seemed to be beating at me, taking control of my mind and body. Why was I afraid? There were so many challenges in life that I could not imagine the ability to overcome. The mind is powerful. It takes control. Psychologists would describe the next incident of fear as an extreme paranoid condition. One afternoon when I was feeling a bit more like getting outside in the nice weather, (still at the hospital rehab unit) my youngest son's mother was pushing me in the wheelchair with our son on my lap. We had to pass in front of the hospital building and there were a lot of people out there. I was scared! I do not know what I was afraid of but I was really scared. I did not have anything on me, like jewelry, so I was not afraid of someone robbing me. Still in all, I thought something bad was going to happen. We turned the corner and I told her to stop real quick. I asked her if she saw what I was seeing and she asked me what I was seeing. "Did you see those two guys running around the van? They are coming for me. They are coming for ME!" She said that she did not see anyone but I continued, "They are coming for me. They are coming for my chain!" Now, I did not have a chain on but I insisted that they were coming for my chain. I told her then to reach down by my wheelchair and get the automatic because if they were going to come near me, we would have to handle this. She reached down and told me that there was not a gun there. Next, I saw a guy walking toward us and I told her that he was one of THEM and was coming for me. The man did not know what was wrong with me and yet I thought this was very real. As he got closer, I shouted to him that he was going to get busted down if he and his boys tried anything with me. I was set in my way so bad that I was tremendously afraid. Having had such a macho attitude earlier in my life, I had to hold my ground and act on what I believed was going to happen. Yes, I thought I was still Mr. Macho, Mr. Man. On the way back to re-enter the hospital, we passed the van once more and I was still convinced that the men were there. My son's mother reiterated that they were not there and finally I realized that I was going through some serious mental changes. Nothing had ever happened like this since I had stopped using drugs, and I knew that I was going to need some help to get over my fears. This was an awakening to the fact that I had to learn how to deal with being in the outside world again but this time as a paralyzed person.

One Wednesday night, there was a group of guys who came to the hospital and came to my room. They heard that I was a cool guy and I had begun to get back a little bit of myself. Some of who I used to be was coming back. They came every Wednesday and soon they just visited with me. I was truly becoming the Damon, with my magnetic personality, that people had known before my accident. These guys told me about their experiences in the chair. Some of them had been paralyzed for ten, twenty, thirty years and were still SURVIVING THE GAME, THE GAME OF LIFE! They truly inspired me to believe that everything would be all right. They spoke of what they had done to survive in a wheelchair and that it wasn't all negative. They made me feel more comfortable. As I thought of what they had experienced, my inner self processed that I too could be mentally fine. They helped me get more emotionally ready for wheelchair life. I began to believe that I could get out of the hospital and make it. Kids in the Hall! That was what they were called. These guys were volunteers who took the time to visit the patients with spinal cord injuries and spread some positive knowledge. They inspired in me the hope for my future as a man in a wheelchair.

Finally, the day came when I was released from the hospital and went to live in Queens. On the weekends, I initially visited my youngest son in Brooklyn. It was so important to me to have time with him, to hold him, help with his feeding, and to interact in a positive, loving manner. He would often fall asleep on those weekend evenings, right on my stomach. I could tell that things were not right with this child's mother but she was going through the motions. It wasn't long though until she broke up with me. She pulled out of the relationship and I had to accept this harsh reality. Some of my family made sure that she had some money to take care of my son and to pay the bills.

Early August was when I left the hospital and that was when my partner and best buddy, the barber, became very sick. He was in and out of the hospital but I never knew what was truly wrong with him. He looked all right and kept telling me he would be fine. He was a tall guy, strong. How could he be sick? I couldn't remember any time he was ever laid up with any kind of illness. I believed he was in the hospital for tests and just never questioned what his symptoms were. I believed that he would be fine and that whatever was the reason for the tests, maybe they would give him medication and he would be fine just as he had told me. He never lied to me. No, we were really tight with each other and had had many wonderful times together both in the work world and socially. When I visited him in the hospital he would say that they were continuing to run tests, that he was on different medications, but he never directly told me what the doctors were trying to do for him. He never said what the diagnosis or prognosis of his condition was. In early fall, I received a call from his girlfriend saying that he had a five percent chance of living until the next day. Yes, my sidekick, my partner, the man I thought I would have as a friend for life, passed from this life into eternal life. His family later told me that nobody wanted me to know that there was no cure for my partner's illness. They knew and so did he that his life was going to be short. He told them not to tell me as he wanted me to get stronger and be able to work and care for my sons.

Now depression set in for a few months as I just could not imagine life without this guy to help me survive. It seemed like there was nothing much left for me. My partner was gone, my baby's mother had deserted me, and here I was, paralyzed. (Nothing more than we could handle!?) I had my children but at that time, nothing mattered. This was the final straw. I said it so many times that truly, this was too much for me to take any longer. I prayed, "Dear God, I don't believe in You anymore. I don't have faith in You. You have given me more than anyone can bear in a short time." Yet, I knew in my heart that my partner, my mother, my friend, nobody would want me to give up.

Since most of his family was from Virginia originally, the funeral was to be held down there. The dark place in my mind which I feared so much was back in my life again. I had to find the power and courage, the energy to do the hardest thing—put my brother down in the ground. They allowed me to speak at his funeral. What words was I to say to bring comfort to this dark and gloomy situation? Words of comfort to the family and to myself? I spoke briefly and from the heart, saying, "I loved my brother and know he wanted me to live. Dear Soul, I'll see you again."

I had to gather every bit of strength and energy that I had to get through each day. I lost the faith and wondered what I had done that was so bad that I had to suffer in this manner. When I sat back and thought about it many days and nights, I began to realize that He allowed His own son to be crucified for the sins of man. Who am I to not take these burdens and SURVIVE? My partner would not have wanted to see me this way. I held my head and tried to understand what the next step would be. I had to try to make some sense out of this whole picture that kept racing before me. One thing was sure. I would need to regain my faith and believe in HIM. It would take some time, but yes, I could do it.

Often I would roll around the old neighborhood where everyone respected me so much, the area where I had grown up. I had to show my face. I knew everybody. I watched the reactions of the people who had known me and had seen me as the macho man. I would stop every few feet as I had to talk to all. When in the car and going down the block, there would be at least thirty or forty people I was waving to and then would stop to say a few words. My friend used to call me the mayor of Brooklyn. I was like the well liked politician. It was ridiculous! Seeing me paralyzed was such a shock to most people and they didn't know what to say. Some shied away from talking to me. Some talked to me and showed me love, but later stayed away. You could feel the distance and know that I was not part of them anymore and I had to accept this, to find a way with which to deal with the issues. Some people would look at me with sympathy, with sadness, and some would actually cry and say, "Oh, I am so sorry." This attitude that people had was not easy for me to deal with as I was still not the strong guy I was before the accident. I was gaining in strength and wanted people to accept me as they had before this tragedy. It was an incredible feeling. Facing the physical problems was one challenge but the emotional stress was a second. In addition to trying to surmount all the difficulties associated with the losses in my life, there were the finances to understand and manage. Before the injury, I lived a healthy lifestyle. There was a good amount of money in my pocket before the tragedy but my world had changed considerably. When I had money, I would give and give and give to anybody who put their hand out to me in need. Now it was an entirely different story. I didn't really expect people to give to me because I always gave from the heart. Life was never promised to be easy and now I was learning this lesson like never before in my years on this earth.

My body had to strengthen before I could reach or even work toward my financial goals. With my advocate and friend at my side, she made sure that the rent was paid for the apartment where we lived, that there was food on the table, and that the daily needs of all were satisfied. She made sure that the proper care was arranged for me while she went back to work. There were home health aides five days a week and I had out-patient therapy at Mt. Sinai to handle my mobility issues. Just going from the wheelchair to a regular chair took a phenomenal amount of strength in my arms and coordination as well as spatial relationships of objects in my environment. "Thank you God for not taking that away." As I recall, there was a special board slipped under my 'butt' and onto whatever chair, couch or bed to which I was moving. This was also true for transferring to the car. Gradually, as I became stronger, I learned to jump from one place to another using my arms as the fulcrum.

When the Mt. Sinai doctors and the therapist team decided they had done as much as possible with transfers, they attempted to have me walk holding onto bars and braces on both legs. My legs were dead weight and it just was not going to work with my other balance problems. My center of equilibrium would not allow walking in this way and possibly never would. Muscles atrophy and nerves die. That is what had happened. However, in my mind I prayed for miracles, but regarding the ability to walk, that miracle did not seem to exist for me.

Spasms have always been a challenge which I have had to understand and learn how to manage. A spasm is a sudden involuntary contraction of a muscle or a group of muscles. It is sometimes accompanied by a sudden burst of pain in some people but that was never true in my case. Spasms are usually harmless and will cease after a few minutes. Many times I have experienced moving from one space to another and one of my legs or both will stiffen and shake. The whole body is slightly affected for a few minutes. This was one of many adjustments.

In addition to the many physical challenges already mentioned, I was faced with not being able to sweat. This is something people often take for granted but for me, it continues to mean I must have a spray bottle of water to keep cooled down in the heat so as not to have heat stroke. When playing any sport, it is also a mandatory piece of equipment. Temperature changes are felt to the extreme and if I am too cold, I will get the shivers. It has happened that even on a very hot day I might get so cold that I need three blankets, doubled, to maintain the proper body heat.

Another physical challenge involves the bowel. This has jabbed my pride to the highest level. For years, I have had to have assistance to get the body waste from the anus. As the years have passed I am able to take care of this function on my own, sometimes with the use of glycerin. Eating and drinking is something I need to be very careful about so as not to get diarrhea. It doesn't take much imagination to realize the unpleasantness of what this could mean to someone who cannot walk. Depending upon where that might happen, it could be very embarrassing but fortunately, it has not occurred too frequently. Then too, weight gain is a major problem which results if there is not enough exercise and the proper diet. Sometimes the body feels so tired that to exercise is a major struggle—it is 'damn' hard. It is so very important to eat a balanced diet but also to eat less and watch carefully not to eat too many carbohydrates. Pushing the chair is much more difficult if you are heavy and need to lift yourself from one place to another. People offer to help but you do not always want that help from an inexperienced person. Spinal injuries are difficult, complicated, and affect so much of one's daily life.

As I became stronger and stronger physically and mentally, I wanted to get on the move more and more. I would push around the park in Queens with a plan to enter the New York City Marathon competitions. As the sun was going down, this was a perfect time to head for the track in the park and push and push. This was an alone time, a time to reflect on what I could do and how to face the many challenges. The ramp and the various pieces of platform which had been built to help get me into and out of the apartment in Queens were very cumbersome. All the parts had to be put in place and then immediately removed to storage. This had to be done by the home health aides or my friend. That apartment building was not handicap accessible. The management insisted that the special-built platforms and ramp were hazardous to other tenants. This was indeed such a burden for those helping me, but it was the only way to feel I was not locked down on the hospital bed in the apartment. Since these ramps to get into and out of the apartment could not be left in place, we decided to look for another living space.

Thus it was that a move to a Brooklyn high rise occurred. No more ramps, and this would mean independence for me. An elevator to get to the apartment level and no more in-house help from Medicaid was needed. This was another freedom earned but now what happens if the elevator breaks down, and it did quite a few times. You are on lock down 'til it is fixed. My psyche had improved considerably but this was what I needed to feel more human and more independent. Still paralyzed from my upper chest down, I had now the strength to push myself around for longer periods of time. And, a special device to drive the car was purchased so I could get a new license and drive myself wherever I needed or wanted to go. Special permits were obtained which made it easier to park nearer the entrances to places I needed to be. This was especially helpful in bad weather but also in many parking lots it was easier to have more space to get around, in and out of my wheelchair.

CHAPTER 6

Fatherhood

Having brought children into the world, I longed to have them near me, and to really be the father so many children do not have. I began to focus on the fact that I wanted to have them be a major part of my life and I of theirs. The boys have different mothers and I had a different visitation schedule for each of the boys. Once I was in Queens, after the hospitalization, the younger boy eventually came to spend weekends with me instead of my going there. Gradually, his time with me increased as I was stronger and could do more with him. After the move to Brooklyn, it was easier to get him and to have him for longer periods of time. He went to preschool near his mother's apartment but entered kindergarten a block from our apartment.

The older of the two boys stayed with me and went to preschool just down the street from the Queens residence. His mother would take him for a day or two, then he would be back with me for two weeks or longer. That seemed to be her pattern in the early days. At one point, she decided to put him in a Christian school in Queens but that did not last very long.

He wanted to be in the same school with his brother and live with me. My intentions have always been to give them as much love, discipline, and understanding of life as their young minds could absorb. As they have been growing, I also have wanted to give them as many experiences as possible.

The mothers seemed strange to me, very strange. They were free to roam, doing whatever they desired to do without the responsibility for what they brought into the world. It never appeared to bother them that they were not the main influence in their offspring's life. Phone calls were at a minimum, which truly has amazed me. It has always puzzled me as to why some women do not have a stronger sense of motherhood. Some women seem to be caught up in themselves and their own world, concerned about their careers, their schooling, and their social life.

Taking care of my children has not always been easy financially. As I mentioned earlier, my friend provided the space for us to live and she provided food as well as transportation. She worked hard to meet all the other needs of the family as well. I had to continue therapy for quite some time and applied for SSI to help out until I could find a suitable job. Since my hands were so messed up, I could not return to work at the barbershop. It was too big a risk that I might get a spasm and make a wrong cut. I did cut the boys' hair, however, and a few friends who would come to the apartment. They truly wanted to encourage me to get back in the business but I could not take the chance.

A major accomplishment for me as a man, a man in a wheelchair with a diagnosed C-6, C-7 spinal cord injury, was when I attained custody of my younger son. It began on one

New Year's Eve when he was with his mother and she refused to let me see him or bring him to be with me. She was quick to argue with me and threatened she would get total custody of the child. There was no way that I was going to let that happen. I contacted a lawyer who was recommended by a teacher I had had in high school, and we met about two times to draw up the case for me to obtain custody of my younger son. My son's mother had a legal aide lawyer who took the stance that I was not capable of raising this child as "I needed someone to take care of me." She used my disability to try to win her case. However, my lawyer had done his homework and proved that I was quite capable, had better housing, a more stable home environment, and needed little help. There were no longer any home attendants from Medicaid and it was apparent in reports that I had earned the respect of many individuals. I was and could continue to be a very respected father. I was awarded custody of my older child through a verbal agreement with his mother, so that both boys could be raised by me. The mothers will always have visitation rights, but amazingly, they do not exercise this right as frequently as one would have expected.

When it came to the child support payments, the younger child's mom was very angry. She resented that I had won in the court. When he needed anything extra, she refused to provide that extra. On the other hand, the older boy's mom has always been willing to give me support for this child's needs and frequently has bought clothes or supplies for both boys.

Since I had no job at that time, I was free to volunteer in my children's school. I had the time to be part of my boys' day-to-day activities. The teachers were very receptive to having me in the school and seemed pleased I was willing to help where they needed assistance. The lunch period was one time in the day that I was definitely welcomed to assist. Classmates of the boys would question why their dad was in the chair. This gave me an opportunity to talk to the students about being in a wheelchair. These children, classmates of the boys, or others who were just curious, showed me great respect.

I became involved with the Parent Teacher Association in the school. There were activities or events at which an extra set of hands and eyes was needed. I helped with many fund raising events such as cake sales, candy sales, and book fairs. I have served as treasurer of the Parent's Association, too. This later led to being on the school Leadership Committee where I served as the chairperson for a term and continue to be a member of that very important school committee. It worked well for the school and for me. The school became like an extended family which gave me support and encouragement. In turn, I also gave the school, administration, teachers, staff, and students my full support. There have been many occasions when I was called upon to speak to a child or children who had misbehaved and needed a man and a father to explain what was right and wrong.

The boys have their own room with bunk beds and dressers I bought for them. Their room looks typical of a boys' room and often needs to be picked up. They need reminding of how to be neat and that everything truly has a place. Age appropriate toys and activities have been provided for them over the years.

Both boys have done very well in school. They have enjoyed learning and had that extra motivation at home. When they needed help, it was always given. They both are excellent readers. As they are growing older, they have the usual tendency to let their minds wander and their concentration wane, and sometimes they neglect taking notes in class. The expectations are high and hopefully they will continue to push hard to achieve their ultimate goals each year.

CHAPTER 7

Involvement in Sports

As the boys became old enough for Little League baseball, they were both enrolled. The youngest was the most interested but gradually his brother donned a uniform and became part of the Mets team at the ball park near our residence. They practiced at that park and had many games there each week. As the second year came around, there was a need for "daddy" help and soon I was a coach. I rolled out onto many a dusty field and coached a base as well. Our team excelled and the boys earned many trophies as a result of their success. As a coach, I received a lot of respect from the parents and the players. Before they could practice, the body had to be ready for the activity. I had a callisthenic program at each practice and then a series of activities which make players stronger and more knowledgeable of the game. My team always seemed to have such a great attitude and showed me that they willingly accepted that discipline. They went from no wins in the first year to twelve out of thirteen the next year and in the third year, the team was undefeated. They lost the championship game, but in their hearts and minds, they were the champions. The parents were always helpful. We went on trips, had barbeques after some games, and enjoyed amusement parks together. The baseball family was unforgettable. I was like a Steinbrenner! Yes, I paid my players when they won. This was a great incentive and proved to be great motivation to be the best they could be.

Again, wanting to be sure the boys had exposure to many activities involving physical movement; they tried football but did not seem very interested at the time. The younger boy enjoyed swimming and the older of the two gradually learned to enjoy getting wet and trusting himself. He needed lots of encouragement and soon found that it was not as bad as he had thought at first. The other sport which they have loved is bowling. Again, it was baby steps, but it was something in which they appeared to have great interest, met many peers who encouraged them and helped them to actually surpass them in ability and league standings. This is one sport with which they have continued the longest interest and participation. They have won many trophies for their efforts both in baseball and bowling.

My further involvement in sports has been really awesome. In 1998, I became interested in trying to play quad rugby. The New York team had come to the rehabilitation hospital and did a demonstration of what the game entailed. Some of the players talked with me and encouraged me to give it some serious thought. Now wheelchair rugby is a team sport for athletes with a disability. The sport's original name was Murder ball but in the United States it has become known as quad rugby. The rules state that a player must have a disability that affects all or a portion of both the upper and lower extremities. It is a very fast paced, full contact wheelchair sport. The game is played indoors on a basketball court. The rules include some of the same or similar parts of other sports such as ice hockey, basketball, soccer, and handball. The physical contact with the manual wheelchair can be brutal. A quad rugby game consists of four, eight minute quarters. There are approximately thirty teams in the United States. The team on which I have been playing has been sponsored by United Spinal Organization and the Jets Football organization. Our team has had to have fund raising events to help cover the cost of uniforms, travel, etc. in recent years. The Easter Seal Society has now become our sponsor. This sport is great for people who are in wheelchairs as a result of various types of accidents. It is an outlet for aggression and fast paced, even strapped in their chairs, there are times that people's chairs are hit so hard that the chair tips over and the player is on the floor. This happened to me a few times but they picked me up and the game continued. Each team has a support staff which helps to get the players in their sport wheelchair and safely strapped ready for action. Because most of the players do not sweat as a result of their injuries, they need frequent breaks for water or Gatorade intake and may need frequent sprays of water.

The rugby season for our team was generally September through April. In recent years, the team has tried to extend the season for occasional get-togethers, social events, and demonstrations or expos. Keeping in shape by doing various exercises is very important in order to be able to push well. Each week the team on which I play practices at Hackensack, New Jersey. I often take my boys and they help me and other players with our equipment or whatever is necessary. Some of the players travel one to two hours each week to get to practice. We run drills and scrimmage among ourselves. This is preparation for the tournaments, about six or seven per season. Depending upon the success in the tournaments overall, a team can qualify for sectionals and perhaps reach the national level of competition.

For me, the benefits over the years have been outstanding. I have been one of the strongest players on the team other than during the first two years. As players age, their shoulders get damaged and they cannot withstand the amount of pushing necessary. Players are classified according to the level at which we function. A point value is assigned from .5 to 3.5. The total of all players on a court at one time cannot exceed eight points. Classifiers generally have medical training such as physicians, physical therapists, or occupational therapists. They are also trained in muscle testing. As a 2.5, I could and do handle the ball well. Since there are four players from a team on the court at one time, two are expected to block or play defense while the other two are offense and are to score. When the opposing team has the ball, then our team must all play defense and be aware of their court presence. Usually each player knows who to defend. For me, having strong arms gives me the ability to move my chair quite rapidly down court. A benefit to me has been that I release a lot of aggression. I face the game as a warrior ready to do battle. When my fellow teammates do the job of defense, the path becomes clear to score. Travel all over the United States has occurred some years depending upon team strength and finances. There were years we traveled west to Arizona and Colorado and south to Georgia and Florida. Generally, we play mostly northeastern teams.

Another benefit of playing quad rugby has been that when we go to tournaments we have a chance to interact with many other people in the same or similar situations as ourselves. We compete for many of the same reasons and, win or lose, there is little animosity off the court. From one season to the next, you look forward to seeing the players with whom you have established a rapport and respect. We pick up the flow of friendship where we concluded at the last tournament. The body and mind are exhausted by the end of a tournament. Tournaments can be one day or can last as long as three days. The benefits definitely outweigh any negative factors.

Another wheelchair sport was introduced to me by my therapist's husband. He has played the sport, wheelchair softball, and found it was also fast paced and enjoyable. For me, the sport is another outlet to feel like a normal individual. I have always been very much an active sports enthusiast. I was frequently seen on a handball court or tossing some type of ball. Participating in softball was another challenge. The rules accommodate the use of a wheelchair with a foot platform but it is played on a parking lot as a field. The players practice weekly and play in summer tournaments. All teams must have a quadriplegic on their team in active play. When the team is hitting, there must be a quad in the batting lineup and bat in the same position throughout the game. The classified quad may alter their bat to improve the grip but that bat must be approved by the head umpire for the sake of safety. A quad may wear a glove on either or both hands and may bunt but must inform the umpire before they are up to bat.

At first, I was really not very good at bat but I have improved. Generally, I am the catcher on the team. My aim is to keep improving and to get a faster push to base once I hit the ball. Paraplegics can do this much faster because of their increased mobility which depends on the level and area of injury. Paraplegics are paralyzed from the waist down. Both lower limbs are affected but they have control of the upper body.

The New York City Marathon, organized by the New York Road Runners organization, is a major annual marathon course covering 26.2 miles. The course event begins on Staten Island near the entrance to the Verrazano-Narrows Bridge. For eight years, I entered and finished this race. What a major accomplishment. As I reflect on this part of my life, it is truly amazing to me that I could push my chair throughout the boroughs and successfully complete the course. We wind through Brooklyn neighborhoods for about twelve miles and at about thirteen and one-tenth miles, we cross the Pulaski Bridge and enter Queens. There are about two and a half miles in Queens and another bridge to cross, this time into Manhattan. The race continues into the Bronx briefly by way of the Willis Avenue Bridge and back to Manhattan over the Madison Avenue Bridge. The marathon ends back in Central Park outside the Tavern on the Green. All along the course people line the streets and roadways cheering us on. The crowd's enthusiasm gives me that adrenalin to push onward. It is so amazing to hear people call out, "GO DAMON, GO! GO DAMON, GO!" or to call out the number on my jersey. Members of my family, friends, and Council for Unity have always been at various points along the way. It is a thrill and "push" to keep moving onward to the finish.

One year, I had a flat tire on my chair and was so thankful for a cell phone to call my brother to bring a replacement wheel and tire. There were different chairs in which I have raced over those years including my regular daily chair, my sport chair, and a hand cycle. The hand cycle is much faster if you have one which fits you well. Each year, no matter what chair I used, I managed to improve my time.

Crossing the finish line is always an accomplishment and a thrill but the greatest excitement is seeing my boys who have waited for me to complete the course. They would ride with my friend, drop me off to go to the starting line, and they would go to Manhattan. There they would get breakfast, sit in the car for a time to read or play some games, and then would head to the area where the wheelchair participants are to meet and greet whoever is there for support. The smiles, the love, the hugs—all have made it worthwhile each year that I entered this incredible race.

CHAPTER 8

Hurdles on the Road to Normalcy

Throughout the years, I have found myself becoming more involved and committed to accomplish what once was thought I would never be able to do. Actually, there are experiences that I never dreamed of doing that have been a reality for me. As my strength increased and my determination to win at whatever goals I set forth intensified, it was like the old adage: "Somebody said it couldn't be done, but he with a chuckle replied, maybe it couldn't, but he wouldn't be one to say no till he tried. So, he buckled right in with a bit of a grin and tackled the thing that couldn't be done and he did it."

For several years I took the boys to Lake George where we rented rooms in a motel. We stayed several days each year and one of my feats was getting in the pool with the boys. My legs are like lead but with assistance, I slowly emerged into the icy cold water and found myself able to float, first holding on to the side and slowly inching away but not far. With confidence and my boys nearby, I showed them and myself that I could swim across the pool. An exhilarating feeling!

Another example of Surviving this Game of Life was when we rented a motorboat and drove it on Lake George. Getting into the boat with some assistance from the owners, the wheelchair was tucked away safely on the dock near the office. Seeing the boys have such fun with a quadriplegic dad was amazing to those who watched or who helped me get in and out of the boat. One thing I wanted the boys to experience is tubing when out on the lake. This is when a large inner tube is attached with a long rope to the back of the boat. The kids get in it and you take off. When you reach a certain speed, the tube begins to lift up from the water. The faster you go, the higher the tube bounces off the water. It is airborne! The object is to try to flip the kid out of the tube but my boys were so scared, they hung on for dear life. This experience occurred during the second year that we were at Lake George. We were about two miles away from the dock when the sky darkened, the wind blew in gusts, and rain began to fall while we were in the middle of the lake. It came in large drops at first and quickly became torrential with huge wind gusts. Pulling them in was a difficult job as I could not get up and rescue them. My teacher friend was petrified to reach out over the open water to pull on the rope. I called to the older boy to jump in and pull the rope to the boat but he too was terrified. The younger one, with my daredevil attitude, jumped in and finessed their rescue to the motorboat. At the dock, my oldest boy was out of the boat first, and the last, of course, was me. The boat owners were quick to assist me and informed us that a tornado had touched down on the other side of the lake. We were drenched but it had been another experience that some physically capable dads do not even attempt.

In the apartment house where we live in Brooklyn, outdoor cooking on a grill is not looked upon favorably. However, at the motel on Lake George there were grills for each unit and that was also something we enjoyed as a family. Whether chicken or burgers, the food tasted so good with dad as the chef. There is something almost magical about the smell of the food cooking on the grill, and then the flavor and taste are so scrumptious.

Should a quadriplegic go camping? Sleep in a tent? Why not? The boys were so excited and loved the whole experience as did I. This was organized by the City Parks and Recreation Department at a park in Queens. There were games of challenge for any or all to participate. The boys loved climbing the wall and watching dad in the challenges he could attempt. Dinner of hot dogs and hamburgers was cooked over an open fire after everyone had set up their tents and organized their little home away from home. The camp leaders took all who wanted to go on a hike in the darkness to have some areas identified and nature explained. When the hike ended back by the campfire, it was snack time: s'mores. The day ended with a very restful night, the boys in their tent and I on a high rise air mattress in my accessible tent. I could roll right in and have plenty of room to go from the wheelchair to the bed. The time went far too fast and my boys once more were so happy to have normal family activities. I think we all felt good to shower and be back home with pleasant memories. The boys were quick to ask, "Will we go again sometime, dad?"

During 2007, I was so blessed to begin a part-time job. This job began as an aerobics instructor at the several beaches where rubber mats had been placed for people who are disabled to get on the beach. I had an opportunity to talk with people, to explain the purpose of the mats, and to demonstrate and encourage various exercises. The position next led to going to several centers where aerobic exercise programs were conducted for people like me and /or seniors who needed that extra support to keep the body moving and muscles active. It has been great for me and I know I have touched many lives and made many new acquaintances and friends. The program has continued at many centers and by December 2008 the number of attendees had more than doubled. My classes were the number one sit down aerobics classes in New York City. Each center wanted more time. This next led to my making a DVD so people can work out at home.

Another first for me was to go hang gliding. Freedom Wings is a non-profit organization run by and for people with disabilities. They operate out of the Van Sant Airport in Pennsylvania. They provide the chance for people who have various physical challenges to fly in specially adapted sailplanes. They give these people the adventure of soaring. Soaring is flying silently. Hang gliders are special planes with no engine. They are towed into the sky by a regular plane. For me, getting in the plane was difficult but there are volunteers present who help. The pilot had me cut the tow line and you could feel the wind take the glider upwards. There were several turns and flips as the natural air currents lifted us. An initial flight usually will last twenty minutes whereas an instructional flight might be as long as two hours. The adrenaline was truly flowing. The cockpit gets hot very quickly but the windows can be opened for air. The pilot was amazed at what I could do. He thought I did so well that I should get my flying license as a pilot. When I could walk, I would probably never have thought about doing this. Flying without a motor? Incredible!

Finally, skiing is another sport I have experienced. When I was walking, this sport intrigued me and I truly loved the experience. There is a special type of ski for the disabled in which you are seated as on a sled. However, two ropes are attached to the back of the chair and two skis attached to the arms. Two advanced skiers are assigned to a disabled individual. They gradually release more and more rope or pull in if the skier has a lack of balance. They instruct you to lean into the turns as you definitely do not go straight down the slope but rather zig zag your way down. To get you on the lift, they lean you back. At the top of the slope, you come out forward and some of us experience "snow face." This is by far the scariest part of the whole sport. Coming down the slope is so very exciting. With adrenaline pumping to the full extent, you don't even feel cold.

The boys were on this ski trip, which was to Bromley Mountain. They loved learning to ski too, and they noticed that not many people of color were on the slopes. It was such an invigorating experience for me to see them come down with eyes sparkling and little fear. They were so excited to see me come down, too, and commented, "Dad can do anything!" These words ring in my ears and are held very dear. It is for myself and for my boys, yes, for all who learn about my struggles that nothing is going to stop me. Nothing will stand in my way which I cannot surmount. Everything takes time, effort, patience and determination.

CHAPTER 9

New Career

After the accident, there was a lot of time to watch television, as life was quite boring when I could not be on the move. Even when I became more mobile, there were the hours needed to be off my derriere and recline to make sure I would not get sores from being in the same spot for an extended time. In the process of searching for entertainment, I watched many comedy shows. As we know, comedy is any discourse that is humorous or meant to amuse. It was so amazing that on all the shows never once did I see anyone in my situation. Everybody was strictly "standup," a single comedian, standing up, with a hand held microphone. I have read that there are or have been a few Caucasian wheelchair comedians, but none who are of color. My mind began to explore the idea as to whether I could be a "stand-up" with humorous made up stories, some based on fact, short jokes and one liners, that would really make people laugh. As a kid I was never thought to be funny. I never dreamed it was possible!

One night I went to the movie theatre near our apartment and there was a table display advertising a comedy show. A local comedian began to speak with me as I inquired about the show and the comedians. After much conversation then, and later by phone, he seemed to think that I was quite funny. I told him I would really like to have a trial run with this comedy scene. This veteran comedian was willing to give me a chance to try my luck at this, another game in my survival tactics. Many hours were spent thinking about what jokes or stories I could tell that would not only make people laugh but would have people wanting to hear more. At comedy clubs, bars, theaters, or wherever comedians entertain, the audience expects to laugh continuously. The performer is under great pressure to deliver "those" laughs. If the performer cannot get laughs, sometimes the crowd will poke fun at the comedian, a practice which is called heckling. How could I get full attention and have people tell their friends that, "this guy Damon is really funny! You have to hear and see him!" It also became a goal to have people see me and others in wheelchairs as people who need not be sad. Most of us do not have the need for Joe Public to feel sympathetic toward us. We want to be living as normal a life as possible.

The first show was in a movie theatre and required having some very strong men lift me in my wheelchair, onto the stage. That stage was very narrow and I knew that I could not move my chair very much or I would be off stage quickly. This is a big problem all across America. There are beautiful auditoriums, places with great acoustics, but the stages are often not accessible. Or, there might be a show scheduled for the second or third floor of a building with no elevator. This is not a very funny part of the life of this comedian as all too often I have been dropped when people are not accustomed to lifting me in the chair. A few times it was easier for the people to take me up to the stage first and then carry the chair. I am not a light-weight individual, so the person carrying me must be strong and healthy. One incident in which I was dropped happened at a Long Island Club. Security was lifting me on stage and I was telling them how to do it. They tipped the chair too far forward and there I was sprawled face down on the stage. Needless to say, this was the ultimate shock to the crowd. They didn't know if this was part of the show or really accidental. It made my job so hard as most people do not find this funny and neither did I. Upon getting in a sitting position, security put me back in the chair and I proceeded with my joking. I had to address the situation immediately or the show would have been a flop. So my opening line was, "If anyone is looking for security to help you, you better save yourself." That opened the crowd right up.

When I have agreed to do a show, whether for a church group, a birthday party, a corporation, or any type of club, it has become necessary for me to learn about the makeup of the anticipated audience. Some cultures would be offended with certain types of humor and I steer away from anything that I think will not be acceptable to the majority of the audience. Sometimes, this is not possible until maybe five minutes before being on stage. Therefore, a comedian needs to have the qualities of flexibility, sensitivity, perception, and a broad range of topics from which the humor can develop. Jokes need to be catchy so that the crowd can be diffused. It is necessary to paint a picture of a scene with words, so that the audience can relate. Of course, the whole delivery depends on my facial expression and body movements. If the show is in a place which sells alcoholic beverages, the following joke is one I might use:

> Most of us can recall a time when we have become drunk, throw up, the room spins and we say, "Lord Jesus, if you let me get through this night, I won't ever do this again." The next night, you are at another club, drink in hand, another and another and the same phrase is repeated. One night, I was at the club and was so drunk, that I stood up. I was all right until the guy next to me said I was standing up. I looked around, "Let me sit down before I lose my benefits. There is probably somebody watching me!"
>
> Another night, I was at a club and had three shots of tequila, two apple martinis, and a Corona. I was messed up! I got in my car, drove home but discovered I left my wheelchair outside the club. How am I getting out of the car now? I was in my car four days. Drove back to the club finally and found three kids playing go-go racer in my wheelchair!

Not all jokes are based on events that really happened, but they have to be easy for people to identify with. There are times my humor does relate to my life experiences in the chair, my children, and even places I have lived. An example follows:

> Anybody here from Brooklyn? (There is always somebody from Brooklyn.) You see, I almost got robbed one night in Brooklyn. Now you know it is really time to move when someone wants to rob a guy in a wheelchair. While rolling down the street, this guy comes up behind

me and tells me to get out of the chair. He keeps following me and says it again, "Get out of that chair!" I turn
around and say, "You don't want my money?" The guy
replies, "No, I'm tired. Just give me your chair!"

Another part of my show business life that is particularly
important to me is the inspirational messages, which are sometimes part of my comedy show. However, there are times I am
called upon to make motivational speeches, which are separate from the comedy. To me, it is so important for people to
understand disability etiquette. First and foremost, we don't
need looks of pity. Even if people feel that, we don't need it
directed at us. I recall when I was first pushing in my former
neighborhood, some folks could not even talk to me without
crying. Some of my family members have had great difficulty
with this too, and it takes time to overcome that overwhelming
feeling of sorrow. Though I am not visually impaired, I share
the message that we need to remember to look directly at the
person and get closer in to their field of vision. The hearing impaired need you to speak clearly and slowly so they can read
your lips. Sometimes when doing a show in a hospital setting
where many people are in wheelchairs or who appear very sad,
or just feel lousy about life, somehow I seem to be able to make
them laugh. As you've read in the previous chapters, my whole
life was turned around by the accident and I try hard to help
people see and understand that you need to have the will to
live. Putting a smile on someone's face is the best medicine for
me. There was a woman in an audience once who will always
stand out in my mind as long as I live. She came into the show,
her tiny body twisted and gnarled and with a very grave look

on her face. At the end of the program she rolled up to me with as much of a smile as she could make, and while not able to truly say words, the sound of her voice expressed the pleasure she had just experienced in my show.

The wheelchair user must constantly be aware of his or her surroundings. Getting in and out of my car can be a hassle depending upon where I am. It is quite necessary to park on a flat surface and not on a hill. People with disabilities need to be efficient and learn independence. My main message is that when somebody has a disability, they need to be appreciative of the positive in their life, what they CAN do rather than concentrating on the negative aspects of life. Being able to smile rather than frown will keep us looking younger and people will be more prone to want to be around us. Laughter is the key to life, so I recommend that people keep on smiling!

CHAPTER 10

Reflections

Life is so precious, but all too often people take it for granted. That was me. Little did I know that experiences in my life would alter my thinking and mature my purposes and goals. When we are infants and toddlers our lives are molded by our parents, grandparents, aunts, and uncles. Then, when we enter school, our peers begin to play a very important part. Family dynamics, siblings, teachers, peers: these people all play a role in developing our minds. Television cannot be excluded. Depending upon what is watched and how much time is spent watching, it can have a positive or a negative impact. As an adult, I came to realize that it takes a strong faith to keep pushing forward each day. My grandmother always said, "God doesn't give you more than you can handle!" During my early years and then especially after the accident, I wondered how I could truly survive, as it seemed too much to handle.

Why all the challenges when just one can be overwhelming? While recovering and in physical therapy there were all the challenges of mobility and learning acceptance of the plight of being in a wheelchair. During that time, I was challenged by the loss of my soul, my friend with whom I worked side by side. At the same time, my one son's mother decided she had no time for a man in a wheelchair. These were huge challenges, obstacles on the path of my life, which had to be overcome.

In the phase of life wherein I became a father, there were more circumstances to ponder, decisions for my sons' well being which had to be made. This is an ongoing, day-by-day role. It takes time to be a caring, concerned father. People frequently make me feel very good when they compliment me on my involvement with the boys. More than once, I have been praised for doing more with my boys than some men who are more physically able.

As a man in a wheelchair, it is hard to rank the challenges I face daily, so I will try to paint the picture succinctly. Eating properly and not gaining too much weight is extremely important. I really eat most everything, but with little activity weight gain is a side effect that is not desirable. Personally, I know that I should exercise more but it is difficult sometimes to mentally equip myself to get the right exercise daily because the struggle is so damn hard. Right now, my stomach is the big problem. I have to watch more carefully what I eat, and perhaps eat less frequently, but eat a balanced diet. Pushing the chair is much more difficult if you are heavy. Also, if you are trying to lift yourself to transfer from one place to another, it is easier if you are not a heavyweight. Not being able to stand up to let the blood flow up and down is a disadvantage. The muscle mass in your legs and stomach diminishes. The psychological factor cannot be minimized. I had a chair in which I could rise to a standing position but it broke at one of my local comedy shows when a very obese woman wanted to sit on my lap and landed in such a way that the chair could no longer be used. Being that I am not wealthy, this presented a problem for replacement. Wheelchairs cost thousands of dollars. So far, it has not been possible for me to replace this type of chair as so many other needs exist for my family.

It has been my good fortune to have my teacher and friend with whom my sons and I could live. She not only has helped to raise them, changed diapers, etc., but was truly a surrogate mother. As the boys grew and attended preschool, she was there to be sure they were going to have a good educational beginning. Once they were attending elementary school, I could volunteer at the school and check that they were doing all right. At home, they had the teacher who showed them so much love and attention. It was second nature to her to instill in them the proper study habits, to have them complete their homework, and to tutor them when and where there was a need. There have been many reports she helped them research, and the results have always been outstanding. This phenomenal woman taught them many life skills. As they were getting to middle school age, she made sure they knew how to do the laundry, could iron, clean their room, and make their beds. The youngest was also interested in learning to cook and bake. They have been normal boys and sometimes have not measured up to her expectations or mine, but they have shown what they really can do. They are truly two wonderful boys, becoming young men.

One thing is certain, her influence in their lives will be there forever.

When my friend retired from teaching, it was necessary for her to move on to be near her family upstate. This was a blessing for her. For me, I had mixed feelings. For her to have an influence on her grandchildren was going to be wonderful and I truly felt good for those little ones. But it was sad and difficult for me to lose this daily support and I have had to make many adjustments. I had grown so comfortable with how she treated me, how she helped raise the boys, how she kept our home, and all the provisions she made for our family because we were and are her family, too. However, I have come to see that miles do not change how someone can care for you. We talk nearly every day at least once and sometimes much more. We encourage and help each other through the tough times and share our joys.

Every day I try hard to keep my spirits high, to keep the determination to make something good happen and to continue to put a smile on someone's face. The smile that is frequently seen on my face is because I am not a quitter. Surviving the game of life is hard work every day, every week, every month, and every year in order to achieve my goals, which will see me ascend to the highest level possible. Meeting the needs of my children and myself is a daily given. Dwelling on the past will not benefit anyone, but learning from the past is essential. Centering on the mental, physical, and emotional pain will not make life better for us.

Helping people to be aware of the type of situations I have survived might be my real calling in life. It makes me feel good when encouraging others in their varied circumstances. Hopefully, I can continue to make a difference in people's lives, giving them a little extra strength to achieve whatever they need in order to make it in this world.

All through life we have experiences, situations, relationships, friendships, and acquaintances. Each person we meet leaves a little of themselves. Some people are placed in our lives for but a moment and others have a lasting, more durable influence. For all who have walked beside me down the major highways of my life, who have been there, believed in me, who have seen my potential in all walks of this life, I thank God. That these individuals have chosen to support and uphold me so that I survived, I thank God. In my quest for a continued most amazing life, I am thankful that even though some of the people who have influenced me have passed from this life, I have their memory instilled in me. Then, a huge influence is promised and will continue to encourage and support my boys and will support me with an eternal presence that is truly staggering.

One chapter ends and another begins all through life. After we are born, stages of infancy, toddler years, elementary years, teens, young adults, middle age, senior, and golden age are experienced. As I have entered middle age, I offer this prayer:

> *Dear Lord, you have created a universe that is so incredible. We can look up at the night sky, see the moon, the stars and sometimes the planets. The amazing creation of this world and all your people in it, is mind boggling.*
>
> *You have given us the tools to survive here, but it has been difficult for me and for many. Each day there are trials and*

challenges. In my life, I have wondered why you kept me here and as I am going through this life, I am beginning to understand. I ask, if it is your will, to help me make a difference in this world and to have the strength to carry on. I want to survive and be the best man I can be. Please forgive me for the wrongs I have committed against you and others. I am oh so thankful for the strong influence of my mom and special friends. Life has taken me through many changes and molded me into the person I am today. Now I want to continue upward.

Dear Lord, please help me knock down all barriers and rise to that individual I am within my heart. I want to be a productive and contributing citizen to my communities. Help me always to be humble, patient, kind, respectful and to toss aside anger and intolerance. Lord, please help me share my talent and help others to be positive in a very troubled world. Help me, O God, to keep the smile on my face and to have the knowledge, the finances, and the ability to protect, guide and advise my sons. May they learn from their father's new life, to survive this game on the path we walk each day. AMEN.

In America, all things are possible. Martin Luther King, Jr. dreamed that one day all would be equal. Barack Obama had a dream and became the first man of color to be president of this great land. I, too, dream that my future success as a person, a black man in a wheelchair, will "bring the house down" on stage and off stage, raising awareness for understanding and peace among all.

Ted Kennedy Jr. made the following recollection at his father's funeral: "Profound losses are survivable—it is what we do with that loss, our ability to transform it into a positive event." This truly sums up the life I have survived. Love and encouragement are necessary ingredients in the equation of success. We need to think positive about our life and not waste energy on negative thinking. This then is the way to Survive the Game of Life.